THE DISSIDENT REVIEW

VOLUME II

FRONTIERS

Copyright © 2023 by The Dissident Review.

All rights reserved.

All images public domain, via Wikimedia Commons.

WWW.DISSIDENTREVIEW.COM

ISBN: 9798398106435

TABLE OF CONTENTS

Introduction	1
In Defense of the Age of Exploration	4
The Inevitability of Conquest	50
The Furthest German	72
William Shakespeare: American Founder	84
Veni, Vidi, Vici	102
Ethnogenesis and the American Longrifle	112
Justice and Force in the Frontier	128
Chuck Yeager	150
Cornstalk's Curse	160
The Memoirs of Rafał Gan-Ganowicz	180
The Trauma of the Frontier	198

INTRODUCTION

"Towering genius disdains a beaten path. It seeks regions hitherto unexplored. It sees *no distinction* in adding story to story, upon the monuments of fame, erected to the memory of others. It *denies* that it is glory enough to serve under any chief. It *scorns* to tread in the footsteps of *any* predecessor, however illustrious. It thirsts and burns for distinction; and, if possible, it will have it."

-Abraham Lincoln, *Lyceum Address*

Today, the past is controlled by an academic elite which has abandoned its purpose: the search for truth, and the expansion of human knowledge. Instead, fanatics run our institutions of learning, and they have replaced truth with ideology. Dissent is not permitted in their journals.

The Dissident Review changes that. Our mission is to publish controversial, banned, and subversive historical research. We require no credentials and publish solely based on merit — because self-education, led by love of what you study, is the only education that matters. We aim to cultivate that education, and give a voice to the massive untapped talent that exists outside of academia.

The academic establishment has forbidden the pursuit of truth, deeming it offensive and dangerous. They fear it because history does not support their ideas. Their shallow perversions of the historical record crumble under the slightest scrutiny. Our goal is to rekindle the spirit of decades and centuries ago, with research not hindered by modern ideology. Merit will once again be able to speak for itself.

In short, we offer a voice to those who wish to challenge the mainstream.

Volume I of The Dissident Review was dedicated to reclaiming and revitalizing the past. We aimed to bring new life to history, a field so dominated by ideologies with destructive goals. This mission remains at the forefront in Volume II, and we are proud to present this collection of historical writing from outside the liberal worldview.

In Volume II, we decided to focus on a particular historical theme, one that is often disparaged by such ideologues: the frontier. The works in this edition particularly examine the spirit of the frontiersman, the "towering genius" described by Lincoln. One who refuses to settle for what is already known, already conquered.

This concept – the call of the frontier – is integral to a proper study of history, and particularly to Western history, where it has defined the rise of so many nations. From the military expansion of Rome to Manifest Destiny in the United States, great men and great nations have been defined by their lofty goals and adventurous soul.

Thank you to all the writers who submitted their work, and thank you, reader, for your support.

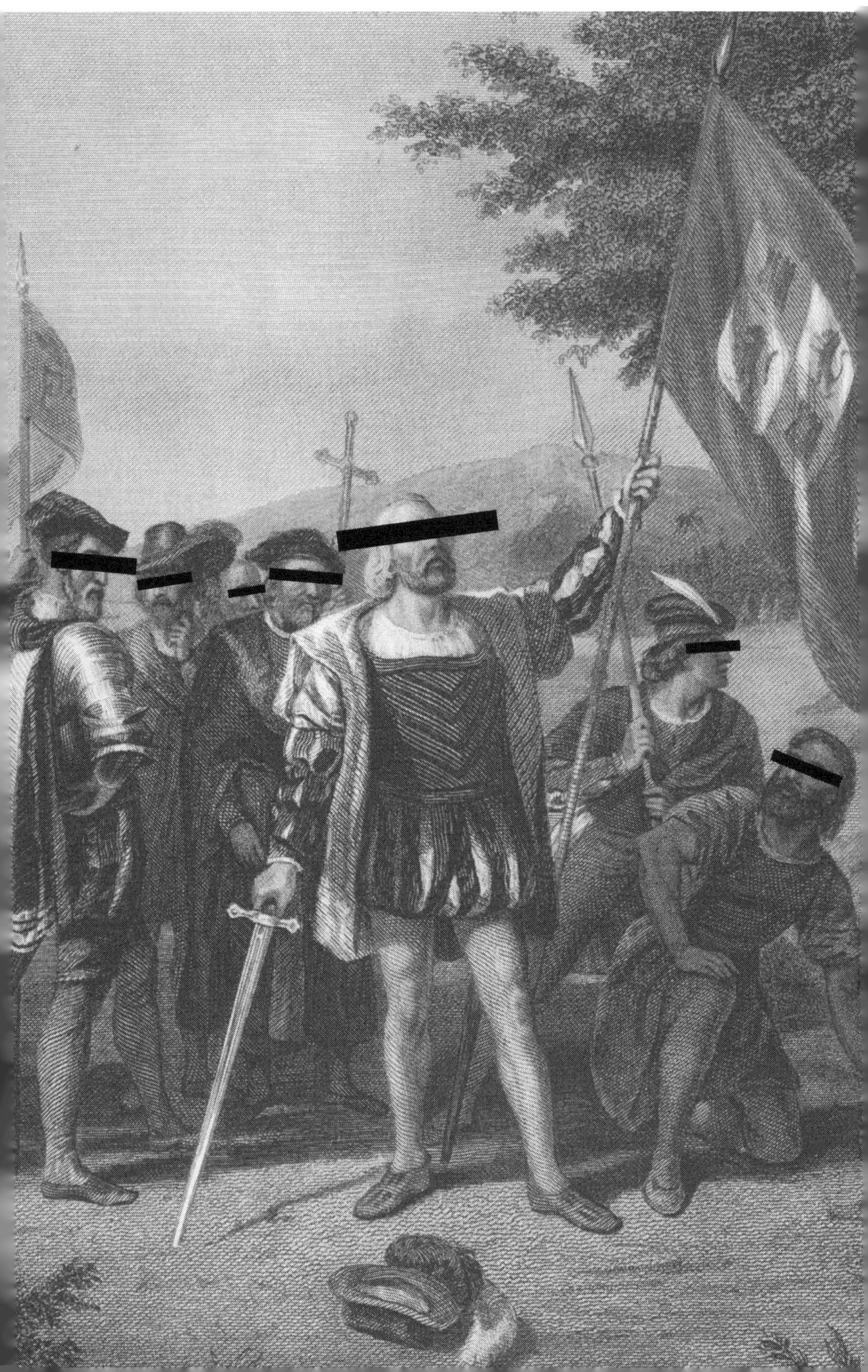

In Defense of the Age of Exploration

By Alaric the Barbarian

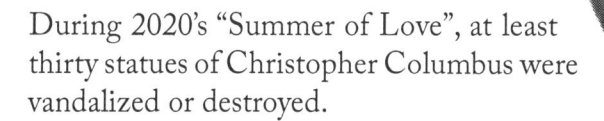

During 2020's "Summer of Love", at least thirty statues of Christopher Columbus were vandalized or destroyed.

Huge crowds surrounded monuments to the explorer, dragging them down with ropes and spray-painting slogans on the rubble. News outlets found this quite inoffensive, even a relief. A Bloomberg headline from those months, instead of lamenting the destruction, reads "Why are there still 149 statues of Christopher Columbus in America?"[1] Dozens of others echoed this sentiment – "it's about time." In cities where riots had flattened storefronts and historical monuments, officials gave trite speeches about "decentering white supremacist symbols," "platforming BIPOC voices." Removing statues of Columbus was painted as an objective moral good, even an imperative.

These speeches and articles provided very little reasoning for their claims, only citing "discomfort" and "historical prejudices." Similarly, articles refer to the change from Columbus Day to "Indigenous People's Day" as already settled, something that is no longer up for debate. The reader is simply expected to understand that Columbus was an evil man, who should be looked upon with scorn; that the early explorers of the New

World were reprehensible figures. To look upon them with anything but derision is passe, even dangerous. One is expected to know that any discussion not based on this consensus is beyond the pale.

But this perspective on Columbus and his contemporaries is a new phenomenon, and its rapid, unilateral acceptance in education and mass media points to nothing short of a propaganda effort. Here, I will attempt to trace the origins of this concept, deconstruct it, and offer an alternative frame; a view of the explorers and conquistadors more consistent with historical truth, and just as importantly, one that provides inspiration and pride rather than scolding derision.

To that end, it is worth stating my position early: Christopher Columbus was a pioneer and a hero, a man we should strive to imitate rather than vilify. The story of the conquistadors is one of the most impressive military conquests in human history, and names like Cortés and Pizarro should rank alongside Alexander and Caesar. These men were model of vitality and sheer will. Bringing civilization to untamed lands is an objective moral good, a Faustian endeavor.

If you were educated in the past 40-odd years, it is likely that most everything you were taught about the Age of Exploration is propaganda. To counteract this, we must purge all vestiges of disdain for the founders of the New World, for ill will directed at them is nothing more than a cheap attempt to undermine America and, more broadly, Western civilization. It is a cheap form of self-flagellation by the most histrionic elements of the Left, a cancerous idea which they have successfully exported to conservatives – who, in an attempt to "compromise", only further their destructive goals.

When communist propaganda outlets are doing their best to make you hate yourself and destroy everything your ancestors have built, there is no "compromise." Instead of finding a "middle ground" between civilization and destruction, we should uncompromisingly defend our historical heroes.

Let us begin.

I

Howard Zinn: Plagiarist & Propagandist

There is perhaps no individual who has done as much damage to modern historical thought as the communist Howard Zinn.

Zinn's 1980 work *A People's History of the United States* crystallized decades of Marxist historical revision into one book – a polemical diatribe against America, the West, Christianity, and more. Written in a tone of haughty revelation, it gained instant popularity among leftist students, who felt that they were reading "the history that their teachers were hiding from them," that they had been shown what's behind a centuries-old curtain of academic conspiracy. Zinn boldly claims to tell the real history of America – America from the bottom up, from the oppressed and subjugated masses. *A People's History* quickly became a sort of Bible for communist historical thought, and elements of it filtered into the public discourse. His view, subversive at the time, is instantly recognizable today as the debased foundation of all post-Zinn historical discussion:

> My viewpoint, in telling the history of the United States, is different: that we must not accept the memory of states as our own. Nations are not communities and never have been. The history of any country, presented as the history of a family, conceals fierce conflicts of interest (sometimes exploding, most often repressed) between conquerors and conquered, masters and slaves, capitalists and workers, dominators and dominated in race and sex. And in such a world of conflict, a world of victims and executioners, it is the job of thinking people, as Albert Camus suggested, not to be on the side of the executioners.
>
> Thus, in that inevitable taking of sides which comes from selection and emphasis in history, I prefer to try to tell the story of the discovery of America from the viewpoint of the

>Arawaks, of the Constitution from the standpoint of the slaves, of Andrew Jackson as seen by the Cherokees, of the Civil War as seen by the New York Irish, of the Mexican war as seen by the deserting soldiers of Scott's army, of the rise of industrialism as seen by the young women in the Lowell textile mills, of the Spanish-American war as seen by the Cubans, the conquest of the Philippines as seen by black soldiers on Luzon, the Gilded Age as seen by southern farmers, the First World War as seen by socialists, the Second World War as seen by pacifists, the New Deal as seen by blacks in Harlem, the postwar American empire as seen by peons in Latin America.[2]

History as told by the losers; by the weak… by the dysgenic and uncivilized, who are held up as bastions of morality in contrast to the supposed evil of the well-turned out, beautiful, and civilized. Nietzsche called this slave morality. Today, it is an easily recognizable, pedestrian expression of leftist resentment.

It is in Zinn's work that we see the first popular portrayal of Christopher Columbus as a genocidal, greedy maniac. All debate on the conquest of the New World since 1980 draws entirely from Zinn's take on the subject, comprising the first chapter of his work. In it he roundly condemns Columbus as a murderer, torturer, slaver, rapist… and an idiot. An incompetent navigator who ended up searching for nonexistent gold to appease investors, using violence where words failed. Zinn sensationalizes the brutality of Spanish rule, how they "hunted natives with dogs," raped and pillaged indiscriminately, and "hanged or burned alive all those who fought back" against their apparent fool's errand for gold. He then extrapolates this view to Hernán Cortés, Francisco Pizarro, John Smith, and other settlers of the New World, all of whom apparently had no higher aims than complete genocide.

In Zinn's perverted version of the Age of Exploration, Europeans sailed blindly into the distance with swords in hand and guns loaded, their bloodshot eyes searching the horizon for the first sight of land which they could pillage and debase. The discovery of America, the founding mythos of the New World, became not a tale of pioneering spirit but rather a sort of original sin, relegating all American civilization to tainted byproducts of genocide. He explicitly frames it as such: "Thus began the history, five hundred years ago, of the European invasion of the Indian settlements in the Americas. That beginning… is conquest, slavery, death." He ascribes this uniquely European evil to greed, and not just simple greed but "frenzy":

> …the frenzy in the early capitalist states of Europe for gold, for slaves, for products of the soil, to pay the bondholders and stockholders of the expeditions, to finance the monarchical bureaucracies rising in Western Europe, to spur the growth of the new money economy rising out of feudalism, to participate in what Karl Marx would later call "the primitive accumulation of capital."

In recent decades, this Marxist drivel has become the foundation for all public education on the Age of Exploration, and the unquestionable basis of all public debate on the matter. Despite the pleas of scholars – both Left and Right – who recognize the academic dishonesty of Zinn's work, it remains at the forefront.

And dishonest, it is. Nearly every quote is manipulated, every fact slanted, every sweeping generalization made in bad faith.

But as we begin our examination of Zinn's dishonest scholarship, it would be bad form to lift points and phrases from another author and avoid giving them credit. So, I would like to acknowledge here that some of the following criticisms – namely the elements about Zinn's primary-source quote manipulation – are not originally mine. They have been drawn from the excellent scholar Mary Grabar, in her paradigm-breaking work *Debunking Howard Zinn*.

I have chosen to mention this reference in the text rather than the bibliography simply because it is a courtesy that Zinn did not extend to his colleagues, whose ideas he "very liberally paraphrased" without credit. In fact, his criticism of Columbus was lifted almost in its entirety from Hans Koning's 1976 work *Columbus: His Enterprise – Exploding the Myth*. So, not only are his points weak and outright propagandistic – they were also stolen. Grabar exposed the plagiarism in her book, beginning with this damning passage:

> The text on pages 1-3 of *A Peoples History*—Zinn's opening narrative about how Columbus cruelly exploited the generosity of the Arawaks—is paraphrased mostly from *Columbus* pages 51-58. From the middle of Zinn's page three to the middle of page four, he follows Koning's pages 59-70; then on the bottom half of page four and the top half of page five, he uses Koning's pages 82-84. Zinn lifts wholesale from Koning the very same quotations of Columbus. He also includes an attack on the historian Samuel Eliot Morison, just like Koning—complete with references to the Vietnam War.[3]

In later chapters, Zinn would go on to lift ideas from Yale professor Edward Countryman, whose work was not even listed in the bibliography of *A People's History*.

It is for this reason that engaging with Zinn "in good faith" is impossible. His work was dishonest, his motives were purely political, and his methods were condemnable. This is incredibly common among so-called subversives; if you're going to write leftist agitprop, at least be *original*.

But originality aside, the points themselves fall apart under scrutiny. This begins with the very first quote Zinn uses, allegedly a damning description of Columbus' sordid motives, written by his own hand in his log:

> They... brought us parrots and balls of cotton and spears and many other things, which they exchanged for the glass beads and hawks' bells. They willingly traded everything they owned... They were well-built, with good bodies and handsome features... They do not bear arms, and do not know them, for I showed them a sword, they took it by the edge and

> cut themselves out of ignorance. They have no iron. Their spears are made of cane… They would make fine servants… With fifty men we could subjugate them all and make them do whatever we want.

When compiled like this, it's quite the condemnation. However, Zinn's ellipses are doing some heavy lifting, to say the least. Whereas ellipses are traditionally used to exclude few words irrelevant to the point, Zinn uses them to exclude entire *paragraphs*, even drawing from diary entries days apart. Like most of Zinn's quotes, this is a cobbled-together mess of out-of-context sentences. The initial description ("well-built, with good bodies and handsome features") is entire paragraphs apart from "they would make fine servants." In fact, the latter quote is only an elaboration on a completely separate observation. From Columbus' log:

> I saw some who bore marks of wounds on their bodies, and I made signs to them to ask how this came about, and they indicated to me that people came from other islands, which are near, and wished to capture them, and they defended themselves. And I believed and still believe that they come here from the mainland to take them for slaves.

Thus, the quote "they would make fine servants" is a deceptive use of translation, further alienated by being taken out of context; in the original, it was only speculation about why these natives in particular must have been valued by neighboring tribes as slaves. And then, the sentence which follows the next ellipsis is taken from an entry two days later! With these words, instead of writing some evil plan, Columbus was remarking on the Arawak's communitarian lifestyle, something he found alien and savage – and of course, something that Zinn elevates as a moral good.

This is another powerful myth that began with Zinn. The idea of the peaceful native; the progressive and nonviolent Indian, who lived a life of perfect tranquility and had no notion of European brutality. This was an incredibly new viewpoint in

American thinking. Within Zinn's lifetime, the Indian Wars had existed in living memory – brutal guerilla conflicts characterized by civilian raids, torture, and scalping. But Zinn disregards this, and instead elevates the Amerindian natives to some sort of proto-communist feminists, who were corrupted by the intrusion of European backwardness and barbarity, most particularly by the detested introduction of Christianity. In his slander of Columbus, Zinn makes sure to paint the natives as contemporary progressives: they had "no churches, or at least no temples"; they practiced free love; their women had abortions at will; they lived in harmony with the earth; they never went to war "on the orders of chiefs or captains." These points are made via selective quoting from Bartolomé de las Casas, himself a hyperbolic and untrustworthy chronicler, and are meant to elicit a very particular conclusion – one that Zinn never outright states, but throughout his book leads readers to again and again.

This conclusion is that "natural life" is inherently progressive, inherently socialist. That Western civilization was uniquely evil for having developed the sins of *prejudice*, and *class*, and *capital*. Zinn holds a deep hatred for European and American civilization, and while he refuses to outright say it, this is the conclusion that he wants his readers (impressionable young students) to draw. The entire goal of *A People's History* is to instill in the youth the belief that all of human history has been the struggle between "the people", who just want peaceful communitarian living, and evil Western aristocrats, who plunge the world into suffering and injustice for material gain. It's communist propaganda, clear as day, which is unsurprising coming from Zinn – an open communist himself.

In order to push this propaganda, Zinn deduced that he would need to make readers hate their ancestry, and draw no pride from any element of Western civilization. To Zinn and his sycophants, Western civilization is a blight on the world, a destructive force that needs to be eliminated. So, heroes like Columbus or Cortés need to be defamed and destroyed in the public eye. One must assume that this is how he justified to himself the brazen lies he wrote about Columbus and his contemporaries: "the ends justify the means." Columbus stood as a symbol of Western greatness, an embodiment of the frontier spirit – and for that reason he had to be destroyed.

However, this entire ideology falls flat in the face of historical truth.

The natives were distinctly *not* peaceful and communitarian. In fact, they were brutally savage toward each other, long before "the white man pushed them to violence," which is Zinn's explicit framing. Wars and slave raids between tribes were common, often including ritual cannibalism – a barbaric and shocking practice to Columbus and his men. Zinn, of course, excuses these by saying "casualties seemed small," and later pointing to them as "violence between groups of the oppressed." In his view, violence is always justified when "oppressed groups" do it, but always detestable when Europeans do it.

Another omission comes in his glowing prose about the natives' peaceful progressivism, which excludes details about Arawak sexual morality, or rather the lack thereof. It wasn't quite the feminist paradise he portrays; girls as young as eight were offered to Columbus as gifts, with assurances that they were virgins. Horrified at the proposition, Columbus had them fed and clothed, and returned them immediately. Immoralities like these among the natives were suppressed by the explorers, which Zinn ignores and other historians depict as some kind of travesty. Generally, when leftists lament the "destruction of traditional cultural practices," this is the sort of thing they're referring to – disgusting, violent, or immoral native practices banned by European Christians.

This is one of the many cases in which Columbus and his men acted completely morally, which of course are absent from Zinn's diatribe against him. In fact, Columbus' first priority, above any notion of repaying his investors or securing resources, was to ensure the conversion, salvation, and safety of the natives.

Columbus took slaves as a matter of course – as was practice among even the primitive tribal peoples he encountered – but he was primarily concerned with their well-being and conversion to Christianity… far different than Zinn's image of working them to death for hallucinated gold. Additionally, he on many occasions ordered his crew to treat them kindly; Zinn omits this, and includes instances of poor treatment *in direct defiance* of Columbus' orders as an indictment of the man himself, implying that Columbus sanctioned meaningless abuses against the natives. He even places Columbus at the center of fantastical orgies of violence, with mass beheadings and slicing of limbs. This is factually untrue, and unsupported by Columbus' log or even the histrionic account of Las Casas.

I could continue breaking down Zinn's narrative for many more pages, but it would be trite. The important point to realize is that Zinn's "takedown" of Columbus – the basis of all modern debate on the Age of Exploration – was an outright lie, a plagiarized work of incredibly dishonest scholarship. More importantly, it was *propaganda*, rhetoric entirely aimed at destroying all positive connotations of the American founding, Western civilization, and Christianity. This extends to his coverage of other conquistadors and settlers, who he doesn't even bother to cover in depth. He recognized the cultural significance of Christopher Columbus, and knew that if he skewered that symbol, the rest would fall in turn. This lie became a perverted version of Genesis for the new Left; a story in which White Europeans committed the true original sin, polluting the Edenic New World with their evil ideas of *capital* and *conquest* and *Christianity*.

It is a blatant lie, from people whose only goal is to make you to hate yourself and give up on everything you stand for. That alone should be good reason to discard it in its entirety.

II

Recontextualization

Even with all of this said, modern propaganda works like a fungus, not a plant. One cannot merely "kill it at its roots" and watch as the rest withers away. In the forty-three years since Zinn's deceptive attack on Columbus, a distaste for the Age of Exploration and its heroes permeates throughout American culture, taking many subtle and differentiated forms.

In particular, Zinn's anti-Columbus stance is expanded along different axes, usually ahistorically and as a mere rhetorical convenience. As in Zinn's original work, the *cause* takes precedence over the truth, and facts are manipulated to make sure that no one, under any circumstances, has a positive view of the Age of Exploration.

One example of an expansion made out of rhetorical convenience is the notion that Columbus was a poor navigator; that the conquistadors were poor fighters and tacticians; that the Age of Exploration was undertaken by men of no particular strength, intelligence, or will.

This argument is appended to the typical moralizing in order to prevent what I call the "Viking effect" from taking hold – that is, the modern idolization of a group *despite* its brutality. This refers to the limited cases in which leftists will permit the valorization of conquest, where the aesthetic virtue of the warrior is allowed to overtake concerns about morality and progressivism. This positive perception of "anti-progressive" cultures is allowed to an extent which directly correlates with the culture's distance from modern Western civilization; thus, the Spartans and the Romans and the Vikings can be seen as "cool" warrior cultures, but perceiving the conquistadors in the same way is not permitted. A similar standard is applied to medieval knights, for similar reasons – but it seems that the conquistadors get a particularly bad reputation as bumbling idiots.

Of course, this was not the case. Columbus' name was once a symbol of naval adventurism and the pioneer spirit for a reason. His voyage was an act of navigational genius and vital risk-taking. He was a frontiersman in the truest sense, venturing into the unknown for glory and the thrill of discovery. The most comprehensive biography of Columbus, *Admiral of the Ocean Sea* by Samuel Eliot Morison, captures the spirit of his discovery well:

> Other discoveries there have been more spectacular than that of this small, flat sandy island that rides out ahead of the American continent, breasting the trade winds. But it was there that the Ocean for the first time "loosed the chains of things" as Seneca had prophesied, gave up the secret that had baffled Europeans since they began to inquire what lay beyond the western horizon's rim. Stranger people than the gentle Tainos, more exotic plants than the green verdure of Guanahani have been discovered, even by the Portuguese before Columbus; but the discovery of Africa was but an unfolding of a continent already glimpsed, whilst San Salvador, rising from the sea at the end of a thirty-three-day westward sail, was a clean break with past experience. Every tree, every plant that the Spaniards saw was strange to them, and the natives were not only strange but completely unexpected, speaking an unknown tongue and resembling no race of which even the most educated of the explorers had read in the tales of travelers from Herodotus to Marco Polo. Never again may mortal men hope to recapture the amazement, the wonder, the delight of those October days in 1492 when the New World gracefully yielded her virginity to the conquering Castilians.[4]

In *A People's History*, Zinn takes special care to slander Morison, because Zinn is incapable of understanding the free and wild spirit described in passages like this. In fact, he despises it. The call of the untamed distance, of the open steppe, of the tumultuous sea – these register only contempt in Zinn's perverted mind. The call of the frontier is decidedly un-leftist, unequal, anti-progressive, and thus in communist thought it is despised. Besides, Zinn hates this view because Morison was an *actual* historian, who in his research on Columbus did groundbreaking work by reenacting the explorer's voyage across the Atlantic. Ideologically he found it reprehensible, and personally he resented that he was unable to produce such scholarship. But Zinn aside, it is worth discussing Morison's more balanced perspective on Columbus.

In his voyage across the Atlantic, Columbus entered the unknown, a trip with no clear path and absolutely no precedent; and yet, he succeeded. His goals were myriad, and difficult to understand in a purely modern frame. Yes, he wanted to secure a sea route to Asia for trade, but that is not all. Columbus also aimed to secure allies against the Islamic tide, which Spain had only in living memory managed to push out of Iberia. Columbus wanted to reach the unknown lands that Marco Polo had once walked; to proselytize to the Great Khan and convert him to Christianity, securing Eastern allies with which European Christendom could halt Islamic expansion. This goal undermines modern understandings of the Age of Exploration, as well as fifteenth-century Europe as a whole; in order to understand Columbus' motivation for reaching the East via the West, one must accept the medieval era as having been characterized by a civilizational clash between Christianity and Islam, a concept I expounded in *The Myth of the Dark Ages* (DR Vol. I). While Columbus was raising funds and support for his expedition, the Reconquista appeared to be merely on hold – a bloody conflict which would inevitably rise again. Thus, securing allies against Islamic conquest was a life-or-death proposition, an insurance policy against future Muslim incursions into Spanish territory. Perhaps, Columbus speculated, with enough funding and enough allies, he could launch a new Crusade to finally retake the Holy Land. This was aspirational, but it is telling that religious motives were Columbus' highest ambition; he could have dreamed of conquering all that lie across the

Atlantic, but even when it became clear that he had reached something other than Asia, his "moonshot" goal remained one of religious fervor.

Besides requiring a more nuanced view of contemporary history, accepting this motive requires recognizing Columbus as a pious and "real" Christian – a concept which is seen as laughable by Zinn et al. The voyage to the New World, contrary to what sneering atheists insist in the public square, was in every sense a Christian mission. Even when it became clear that Columbus had not reached outlying islands of India, that mission remained Christian, changing only in methodology.

Columbus' log supports this on multiple occasions. For example: "I want the natives to develop a friendly attitude toward us because I know that they are a people who can be made free and converted to our Holy Faith more by love than by force." This piety is echoed even by the most uncharitable historians. Koning (whom Zinn plagiarized much of his Columbus "scholarship" from) even had to admit Columbus' deep faith: "…in that religious and bigoted age, Columbus stood out as a very fierce Catholic. When he discussed his westward voyage, he always dwelt on its religious aspects…"[5]

Even Las Casas, whose chronicle of Spanish rule in the New World was extensively weaponized by Zinn, admired Columbus' Christian goals and piety. Instead of scorning Columbus, Las Casas lionized the explorer, seeing him as the larger-than-life figure which Zinn would later call a "fiction":

> Many is the time I have wished that God would again inspire me and that I had Cicero's gift of eloquence to extol the indescribable service to God and to the whole world which Christopher Columbus rendered at the cost of such pain and dangers, such skill and expertise, when he so courageously discovered the New World…[6]
>
> Among his natural attributes… [he] was a tall, imposing, good-natured, kind, daring, courageous, and pious man.[7]

The point here is that Columbus *was* a larger-than-life figure; that he deserved his mythologization as the pioneer discoverer of America in the name of Christianity. This is the one fact that Zinn does his best to subvert, the one truth that is most heavily suppressed today.

While Zinn does his absolute best to drag Columbus, Cortés, Pizarro, and similar through the mud, he cannot escape the simple fact that they were *great*, in the ancient sense of the word. By their very nature, these men were "larger-than-life." Their contemporaries described them as awe-inspiring, and the natives they encountered often saw them as gods. They were men of force and vitality, who did *great* things: they sailed off into unknown lands, conquered every place they touched, and spread their religion and language so strongly that there are millions more speakers of Spanish and Portuguese in the New World than the Old. Their motives ranged from starting a new Crusade to finding a city of gold, but all were herculean projects – aspirational goals with charismatic figureheads, each inspiring dozens or hundreds to risk their lives for a slim chance at success. Then, upon landing in the New World with few men and limited supplies, they tamed the untouched wilderness and often-hostile peoples of the Americas. They built forts, towns, and missions; later, these became sprawling cities, beacons of civilization some four thousand miles away from the nearest European harbor.

All modern slander cannot stand up to the fact that the explorers of the fifteenth and sixteenth centuries are some of the most impressive people in history. Their lives would stand as great if told to an ancient Greek, Roman, Assyrian, or Mongol. There is in the Age of Exploration a Classical sense of vitality, of excellence and triumph.

This brings us back to the "Viking effect." Because of this innate sense of Classical greatness present in the explorers and conquerors of these centuries, much effort is dedicated to making them seem banal or incompetent, unworthy of special interest beyond scorn. Besides slander of their motives – most often a reduction to the simple drive for pillage – and their religion – by calling their Christianity skin-deep, a mask under which they concealed raw greed – historians and culture warriors have a particular tendency to dismiss the Age of Exploration as being dominated by men who were *boring*... which in historical education is perhaps the greatest sin of all.

But Columbus and the explorers that followed him to the New World were *anything but boring*. Their lives and adventures are worthy of dozens of blockbuster movies, and it is merely politics that prevents their lives from being well-known today. These explorers demonstrated the same drive and talent as Alcibiades or Themistocles, yet have been unjustly filed into the dustbin of history in a blatant propaganda effort.

III

Men, Myths, Legends

With this section, my goal is to provide the rich historical detail omitted from Zinn-style smears of the Age of Exploration. So far, I have discussed much about Christopher Columbus… but for the moment I'd like to highlight some other names, which are too often listed as footnotes to the debate over Columbus.

We will revisit the discoverer of the New World. But I believe that it is important to first highlight some other explorers and conquistadors, simply because their deeds are often obscured – seemingly to prevent any appreciation of the sheer scale of their enterprise and willpower. While Columbus' discovery and conquest can be twisted into a militarily unimpressive and primarily symbolic endeavor, the expeditions of Cortés, Pizarro, De Soto, and others cannot. Ever since Zinn's politicization of this era, the leadership and tactical brilliance of these men has taken a backseat to petty moralizing and scolding condemnation of European exploration – a trend which must be reversed for any meaningful discussion.

So, to counter the propaganda which dominates discussion of the Age of Exploration, recentering the conversation is a necessary step. In order to do that, we must first know the stories of the explorers who conquered and built the Americas. In this section I will focus primarily on the Spanish conquistadors who tamed the Aztec and Inca empires; later essays in this volume deal extensively with the conquest of the North American frontier, so in an effort to avoid repetition, the focus will remain on Spanish conquests in the New World.

CORTÉS

Hernán Cortés was a character worthy of a Stevenson novel.

Born in 1485, just prior to Columbus' first voyage, he experienced a childhood much like dozens of other larger-than-life characters in history, from George Washington to Teddy Roosevelt. That is to say: he was pale, sickly, and harbored unrealistic dreams of adventure. His parents, of impressive ancestry but less-than-impressive means, outlined a legal career for him, hoping that he would return the family to a position of wealth. However, Hernán hoped to follow in the martial footsteps of his father, an infantry captain who had led countless charges against the Moors. As he matured and became healthier, this conflict came to the surface; much to his parents' disappointment, it became clear that he would not follow their desired path. Cortés was destined for a world not defined by statutes and contracts. In his youth, he was described as mischievous, arrogant, ambitious, energetic. Clearly his place was not in Spain, but somewhere wilder – somewhere he could impose his will upon the world.

In early sixteenth-century Spain, the obvious place for this sort of adventure was the New World. Fantastical stories about the untamed frontier had captured the Spanish public, and at only eighteen Cortés decided to make the journey to Hispaniola. Leveraging a family connection to Nicolás de Ovando, governor of the island, he became a citizen and began working as a simple notary in Santo Domingo. However, this position would not last; after volunteering for expeditions and distinguishing himself in the conquests of Hispaniola and Cuba, Cortés rapidly rose in the ruling class of the Spanish territories. By twenty-six he was secretary to the governor of New Spain, and magistrate of Santiago in the newly-acquired territory of Cuba.

The aggressive meritocracy which allowed Cortés to rise to power at such a young age is nearly unfathomable today, in our age of bureaucracy and corporatism. But this ruthless meritocracy was the primary draw of the New World in its early years. The same sense of do-or-die, intense competition would later animate settlers of the American frontier, civil engineers in the remotest jungles of the world, and test pilots for spacecraft; the lawless and unknown fringes always speak to enterprising individuals. The inherent meritocracy of these places is one of the many reasons that young men feel such a strong call to new frontiers; at the edge of the tamed and owned world, an ambitious individual can test himself against his peers and the world, risking everything in a truly open environment.

In the early sixteenth century, New Spain was this frontier – a budding nation where young talents like Cortés could test their mettle and quickly rise in stature. It was in this environment that Cortés excelled. His talents for leadership, rhetoric, and battle set the stage for the acts which would engrave his name in history.

These acts began in 1518, when Governor Velázquez made Cortés captain of an expedition to Mexico. Despite the trust conferred by this appointment, the relationship between Cortés and the Governor was one of extreme tension; Cortés had been romantically involved with two of Velázquez's sisters-in-law and had recently married one, a situation which Velázquez resented strongly, despite his respect for Cortés as a leader. Thus, Cortés' appointment as Captain-General was a begrudging rather than enthusiastic promotion.

After a few days, Velázquez's personal vendetta overtook his professional consideration, and he changed his mind on the appointment. With Cortés' preparations for the expedition barely underway, he revoked the charter and recalled the hopeful explorer.

But Cortés already had his sights fixed on Mexico, and he carried on undeterred, ignoring the Governor's sanction. Hoping to preempt a more serious attempt at reigning him in, Cortés rallied six ships and 300 men in less than a month – an act of recruitment straight out of the pages of the Anabasis. This is where Cortés' skill for rhetoric most clearly shines through; he proposed something impossible (even illegal), and yet men clamored to join his crew, to seek glory in the untamed lands of Mexico. When Cortés' fleet set sail in February of 1519, it was an act of open mutiny… but he continued nonetheless, captured by the potential for greatness.

When the conquistadors reached the shores of modern-day Mexico, they soon encountered another figure whose life deserves more attention: Gerónimo de Aguilar, a Franciscan priest who had partaken in an earlier, disastrous expedition along the Mexican coast.

Aguilar was one of just two survivors of this exceedingly unfortunate voyage, which had set sail some eight years prior. After a shipwreck, he and a handful of other survivors were taken captive by the Maya. There, most of them died of disease or were sacrificed. Before Aguilar's scheduled execution, he and another (a sailor named Gonzalo Guerrero) managed to escape… only to be captured again, this time by a different Mayan tribe. For eight years he lived as a slave, learning the local language and customs. Guerrero did the same, eventually rising to a role of a war chief for the Mayan tribe that had captured both men.

In early interactions with the Yucatan natives, Cortés' men heard word of their fellow bearded Spaniards, and made contact. They liberated Aguilar, and he immediately offered to join Cortés' expedition as a translator.

During eight years of captivity and slavery, Aguilar had never faltered in his religiosity, nor in his observance of priestly duties. Upon meeting Cortés, he was able to correctly state the day of the week based on his schedule of prayer, which had never been broken. By this demonstration, Cortés knew that Aguilar had never "gone native"; that he was a Christian and a Spaniard still, and that he could be trusted to negotiate on his behalf.

Such was the caliber of men who set off for the New World.

Now with a translator and some initial skirmish successes, Cortés' expedition reached Veracruz and claimed it in the name of the Spanish crown – officially placing the group under the jurisdiction of Charles V, in order to circumvent any interference by Velázquez. This legal matter would not stop Velázquez from interfering later, but it gave the expedition a more official sanction as they prepared to march inland.

Through conversations with Aguilar and observation of the natives, Cortés began to understand the sheer scale of Aztec civilization, the vast hostile territory ahead – and therefore the herculean task that lay past the sandy beaches of the Yucatan. His men, drunk on early success, would need motivation, commitment.

So, upon landing on the shores of Veracruz, Cortés made the decision that he would return "with his shield, or on it." It was here that he issued perhaps his most famous order, one that has gone down in history as an example of pure commitment to one's cause:

"Burn the ships."

The conquistadors would return on native ships, or not at all. One can only imagine the impact of the scene, as the conquistadors' only way home crackled and burned against the sunset, thousands of miles from home. Less than a battalion of men made camp on this strange and hostile shore, surrounded by enemies with no possibility of retreat.

The only way out was through. And Cortés certainly went through – he reached the Aztec capital Tenochtitlan in four months, a march characterized by constant battle and negotiation. This military conquest was, above all, an act of strategic genius; between powerful rhetoric and overwhelming force, Cortés' detachment of 500 reached Tenochtitlan in a matter of months, recruiting on the way at least 1,000 native warriors.

Tribes encountered along the way were either subdued or turned against Aztec rule; the latter became an increasingly common occurrence as the Spaniards made their way toward Tenochtitlan. After repelling much larger forces in combat, Cortés would call for negotiation, where he made high promises: namely, freedom from the bloody yoke of Aztec rule. No more imposed human sacrifices, no more taxes paid to bloodthirsty shaman-rulers, no more taking of slaves and women. Instead, Cortés offered local freedom, fantastic cities, and eternal salvation. Perhaps some natives saw him as an emissary of Quetzalcoatl, with his new technology and strange religion; perhaps not. Either way, the Tlaxcala natives certainly saw his men as powerful fighters, and Cortés as a potent ally against the Aztecs. On the march to Cholula and then to Tenochtitlan, Cortés' army snowballed in size and local support.

Historians tend to slander this element of Cortés' expedition, pretending that he lied and cheated to exploit native divides. In reality, he simply offered a better deal than the Aztecs, with a strong assurance of success emphasized by the Spaniards' shining armor and terrifying artillery. He had also gained the respect of many tribes, even those which initially opposed the Spaniards – something that is often difficult for today's effete commentators to understand.

In battle after battle, the strange explorers proved themselves a formidable enemy – and not just due to their technology. While guns certainly made an impact on skirmishes with the natives, contemporary firearms were much more primitive than we tend to imagine. When guns and cannons were used in the New

World, the conquistadors often managed only an initial salvo before the fighting became much more physical.

"The armor, the pikes, the Toledo steel blades, the discipline and know-how from decades of fighting the Moor… and above all, the bravery and daring…"

Bernal Díaz's account of the conquest made it clear that while guns were useful, the Spanish almost always fell back to their swordplay and formation training. Even when "surrounded on all sides," the Spanish repelled each charge, inflicting heavy losses with their superior tactics and arms. Díaz described these melees as "rather hot work", leaving the bloody details to the reader's imagination.[8]

It was in this "hot work," these struggles of obsidian and steel, that Cortés' soldiers proved their mettle – both to Cortés and to the Tlaxcala chiefs that witnessed their prowess. The Spaniard's tactics, standard in Europe, were the result of centuries of brutal refinement, a crucible which had never formed in the New

World. So, when natives launched dispersed, unarmored charges against the Spaniards, it quickly became clear that fighting was useless, and that allying with the Europeans would be far more advantageous than trying to defeat them.

This was a strategy that the Aztecs themselves had been using for centuries: 'We could crush you, but if you choose to join us instead of fighting, we'll help you get rid of those other threats to your people.' Cortés simply did it better. Thus, when he marched on Tenochtitlan to finally meet with Moctezuma, Cortés had behind him an army of Otomis and Tlaxcala fighters, led by Spaniards bearing arms which must have looked like magic to the Aztec capital's populace.

Moctezuma cautiously welcomed the Spaniards into the city, hoping to keep them occupied for long enough to ascertain their weaknesses. This would prove to be a fatal mistake, as negotiations quickly broke down, with both groups becoming guarded in manner and speech. It became clear that the illusion of civility would soon be dropped. The only question was who would throw the first punch.

Cortés decided that he would act first. Despite being outnumbered and confined dangerously within Tenochtitlan – an island of some 200,000 people – he initiated a sudden coup, taking Moctezuma hostage. In one daring move, the Spaniards gained control over the entirety of the Aztec empire. Through bravery, cunning, and force of will, a mere 600 men had conquered millions.

~

However, this was by no means the end of Cortés' struggle in Mexico. His feud with Velázquez soon returned to the forefront. Not long after Cortés took control over Tenochtitlan, the Governor's fleet arrived in Mexico to arrest Cortés and his men for mutiny.

Cortés took some of his forces to meet Velázquez's army, leaving only 200 men to control Tenochtitlan (and by extension, the entire Aztec empire). Outnumbered, outgunned, and running low on supplies, he nonetheless defeated Velázquez's men handily.

In the aftermath, Cortés once again showed his rhetorical skill and personal magnetism: he convinced the force *sent to arrest him* to join him in conquering Mexico!

However, even with these additional men and supplies, securing the conquest of the Aztec empire would take many more months. Soon after Cortés' newly-bolstered force returned to Tenochtitlan, Montezuma was killed by his countrymen; in the chaos which followed, the Spanish were driven out by locals, in a wild battle mainly fought between a floating bridge and hundreds of war canoes. Díaz recounted it as a scene of pure havoc, something reminiscent of the Battle of Salamis – though with the Spaniards as the Persians, accosted on all sides by an ambushing enemy.

However, undeterred by their first and only true defeat, the conquistadors soon besieged, retook, and razed the Aztec city. When they marched on Tenochtitlan for the second time, they did so with a dozen brigantines and some 200,000 native allies, in what was likely the largest battle of the age.

The success of this siege finalized Spanish control of the Aztec empire, and Cortés received official permission from Charles V to rule this new territory. As governor, he went on to rebuild Tenochtitlan as Mexico City, converted thousands of natives to Christianity, and tamed the fractured world of sixteenth-century Mesoamerica in the name of the Church and the Spanish crown.

~

In order to settle political disputes with his countrymen, Cortés returned to Spain twice after his conquest of Mexico. Upon his first visit, he was received by Charles V with honor and distinction; the emperor granted him a coat of arms, official titles, and vast property in the new territory.

But on the second visit, he went unrecognized. After pushing his way through a crowd to speak with the King, the monarch did not recognize him, demanding to know who the man accosting His Majesty was.

"I am a man," Cortés answered, "who has given you more provinces than your ancestors left you cities."[9]

This is the Cortés that the history books should remember.

PIZARRO

Like Cortés, Francisco Pizarro rose out of nothing, but was driven to greatness by the desire for glory and conquest.

In fact, the circumstances of Pizarro's birth were even more austere: he was the bastard son of infantry colonel Gonzalo Pizarro, raised in obscurity by his poor mother and grandparents. He never received any formal education, and grew up working as a mere swineherd in absolute poverty. Because of this simple origin, little else is known about Pizarro's life before his journey to the New World; however, it is likely that he participated in manorial wars and similar local conflicts, perhaps even joining a campaign in Italy. Such a background would help to explain his later military prowess... but again, this is unverified. Perhaps a young Pizarro found a taste for battle in these local clashes, learning strategy and tactics; or, perhaps he was simply gifted with boldness and an inclination toward strategy.

Either way, Pizarro saw the New World as his only chance to ascend beyond his station, and joined an expedition to modern-day Colombia in 1509. Like so many other men of that age, Pizarro wanted to test himself in an environment of pure merit, to be the settler of unknown lands and the discoverer of unseen riches. The New World presented the chance, to test oneself in a place of infinite opportunity and infinite risk. Its call was particularly felt by men like Pizarro, who had higher ambitions than their birth-given station.

However, aside from wealth, the call of the frontier for its own sake was particularly strong in Pizarro. Upon arriving in the New World, he immediately joined campaigns under Enciso and Balboa, diving headlong into the complex world of native alliances and unforgiving nature.

While exploring alongside Balboa, Pizarro became one of the first Europeans to see the Pacific Ocean, a difficult journey with a triumphant zenith. This experience seemed to satiate him for a few years, during which he worked his way up the social ladder of Terra Firma (Spanish territory on the mainland). This single-minded rise to power culminated in his promotion to magistrate and mayor of the recently-built Panama City. It was at this time that Pizarro first heard whispers of Piru, an untouched land of mountainside golden cities – including the famed El Dorado.

He began planning an expedition deep into South America with another conquistador, Diego de Almagro, and a priest, Hernando de Luque. They set off from Panama with too few men and meager supplies, but nonetheless had lofty goals and plenty of optimism.

However, optimism and ambition alone do not make for success. Pizarro's first expedition would end in disastrous failure – as would the next. After a full two years of brutal weather, little food, and belligerent natives, Pizarro found himself waiting on a small island for yet another round of reinforcements.

But this time, they would not come – the governor of Panama, Pedro de los Ríos, had finally declared the expedition a lost cause. When two of Ríos' ships arrived to take Pizarro and his men back to Panama, he rebuked them and refused to be recalled, defending the voyage in a frantic speech: "There lies Peru with its riches; Here, Panama and its poverty. Choose, each man, what best becomes a brave Castilian. For my part, I go to the south."[10]

This act must have looked like insanity; perhaps some tropical disease had eaten at Pizarro's sense of reason. The new arrivals tried to reason with him, but it was of no use – he would not give up on the expedition yet.

A mere thirteen men stayed with Pizarro – a group known today as the Famous Thirteen. This handful of men, drunk on the pioneer spirit, refused to accept failure. They would continue to endure austerity and hardship for the chance of success, of true conquest. After the group sent by Ríos departed for Panama, the Thirteen constructed a boat from local materials and sailed to La Isla Gorgona – an impressive feat of seamanship for what amounted to little more than a raft. For seven months they waited, betting that their sheer conviction would bring more supplies and recruits.

And seven months later, precisely that happened. After much cajoling, Pedro de los Ríos had finally agreed to send a ship to their rescue, with explicit instructions that it would return to Panama in short order and formally end the expedition. However, like Cortés, Pizarro, Luque, and Almagro had little concern for orders to stop their exploration. The voyage would continue south.

It was on this last-ditch excursion that Pizarro and his followers experienced their first success, meeting friendly natives and establishing a camp in Tumbes. Scouting expeditions returned with wild reports of immense wealth and untouched land. The conquistadors had found their inroad to Peru – a land governed by a powerful empire with an apparently resplendent capital, echoing the rumors of advanced, golden cities.

The men returned to Panama with samples of Peruvian wares, but were met with disinterest from Ríos (whose orders they had just spurned). Undeterred, Pizarro left for Spain to appeal directly to royal authority. He impressed Charles V with his stories of rich lands in Peru, as well as his samples of gold and llamas – but after negotiations were put on hold, it was Queen Isabel who would finally sign the charter for the conquest of Peru. Pizarro was named Captain-General of the expedition and charged with raising 250 men: armed, trained, and fit to conquer an empire of over 10 million.

The expedition faced difficulties from the moment they landed in Peru. After an initial skirmish with natives at the Battle of

Puna, they disembarked again at Tumbes. Here, a warm welcome was expected; however, Pizarro and his men found the village deserted and nearly destroyed.

They soon learned from other natives that Punian tribesmen had raided Tumbes – was this retribution for trading with the Spanish, or part of an unrelated conflict? The conquistadors could not tell. This was a sobering moment for the expedition; the land around them was suddenly all the more hostile and unknown, and their planned safe haven at Tumbes would have to be forsaken. The group trekked inland, facing ambushes that could materialize at any moment out of the jungle. Pizarro issued an order to wear armor at all times, causing chafing (both literal and metaphorical) among the men. Skirmishes were a common occurrence, and disease eroded the already-small force. To Pizarro and others who had partaken in the original explorations of the region, this must have echoed their earlier, failed voyages. Supplies were dwindling, the men were unmoored from any support, and the plan went no further than simply marching forward.

Here, Pizarro once again snatched victory from the jaws of defeat. The expedition came upon a midsize village and took it in the name of Spain, naming it San Miguel. This settlement, the first true Spanish holding in Peru, would serve as an important launching-point for the rest of the conquest, and a much-needed place to rest and resupply in the meantime.

San Miguel was also the first *repartimiento* in the New World, a type of governance which would eventually come to replace the encomienda system. Repartimientos were based on tribute labor, and in fact were a direct adaptation of the Incan system already in place throughout Peru. Historians like Zinn tend to describe Pizarro's conquest of San Miguel de Piura as "enslaving the natives," but in reality, the situation was more in-line with a political coup. The natives continued their way of life, as unenslaved peoples that owed intermittent labor to the controlling government.

However, Pizarro soon left the relative safety of San Miguel, seeking an audience with Incan authorities. He left 50 men to govern the town, and advanced with the rest of his forces into the mountains.

It was then that the conquistadors began to learn more about the contemporary situation within the Incan empire. Fresh out of a bloody civil war, the empire had stabilized under Atahualpa, a demigod-king straight from the annals of Antiquity. His armies were well-equipped and numbered in the tens of thousands. Clearly, the immense wealth of Peru had allowed for a prosperous, complex civilization, arguably more advanced than the Aztec conquered by Cortés (both culturally and militarily).

It became clear that a mere show of force would not be sufficient. Pizarro needed something shrewder, more daring.

Thus began a protracted battle of wits between Pizarro and Atahualpa, starting with the September 1532 dispatch of Hernando de Soto to an Incan garrison. Pizarro chose de Soto to make contact due to his demonstrated courage and intelligence – traits which would drive him to later explore swaths of North America, including leadership of the first European crossing of the Mississippi. But here, de Soto was still just a captain and envoy, seeking an audience with a king who controlled a territory the size of a considerable European state.

By this point, Atahualpa had heard reports of the Spaniards: strange men wearing ornate metal armor, carrying weapons unlike anything known to the Inca. However, due to Atahualpa's recent success in the war against his brother, he did not take the Spanish seriously; even with their odd dress and rumored supernatural powers, the small group clearly posed no threat to his massive legions. He regarded them with curiosity, and like Moctezuma, aimed to bring them closer in order to learn more about them (and, if necessary, destroy them).

After a long series of envoy meetings – painstakingly-translated, tense affairs – the situation looked grim for Pizarro and his 180 men. Throughout the negotiations, Atahualpa had drawn the Spaniards increasingly deep into the mountains, promising them a meeting at Cajamarca. An Incan noble guided the conquistadors through fortified mountain passes, features which Pizarro noted would prevent any attempt at retreat. An initial meeting between de Soto, Friar Vicente, and Atahualpa made it clear that the Incan monarch was not willing to capitulate to Spanish demands – but the Spanish nonetheless had to advance inland, to preserve the image of invincibility (seemingly the only factor that had prevented an attack so far).

Their destination, Cajamarca, was a valley town, flanked by mountains which were packed with some 80,000 Incan soldiers. The town's inhabitants had been relocated prior to Pizarro's arrival, and the expedition found the streets eerily quiet – presumably to prepare it for an overwhelming Incan attack.

Here, it became clear that the Spanish had overextended themselves. Any attempt at fighting would be futile, and retreat was off the table due to the easily-blocked mountain passes. Pizarro also noted a time constraint: the longer the Incans could observe the conquistadors, the less scared they'd be of their rumored "supernatural powers." They were trapped in hostile territory and drastically outnumbered. The situation seemed hopeless.

However, even with these impossible odds, Pizarro was indefatigable. Upon their arrival on November 15th, he gathered his officers and devised perhaps the most daring plan of the era.

The Spaniards would capture Atahualpa *from the middle of his forces*. Outnumbered nearly 450:1, the conquistadors needed such a bold, audacious move for any hope at survival – much less victory. However, through subterfuge and the use of shock and awe, Pizarro reasoned that they could once again snatch victory from the jaws of defeat.

Pizarro had invited Atahualpa to visit the next day, and it was then that the conquistadors would spring an ambush on whatever forces accompanied the Incan king. Pizarro's men concealed themselves in alleys and buildings, hiding cavalrymen around corners and positioning their small cannons in windows overlooking the town square. To their great concern, a large segment of the Incan army marched ahead of Atahualpa. In a dramatic turn of fate, the soldiers did not occupy the city, instead setting up camp outside its walls as a show of force. However, this did little to ease the tension among the Spanish, who held their positions in excruciating silence.

The meeting commenced just before sunset. Atahualpa entered Cajamarca with a massive display of wealth and splendor: his retinue of over 8,000 was brightly dressed and laden with gold and silver ornaments. The king himself was carried on a silver, parrot-feathered litter, and the nobles preceding him sang ceremonially.

Only Friar Vicente and a translator emerged to meet Atahualpa, much to the confusion of the Incan procession. Vicente was given a golden cup of chicha, which he did not drink for fear of poison. Instead, he gave the king a missal and proceeded with explaining the Catholic faith. Furious with the friar's apparent insolence, Atahualpa threw the missal to the ground and threatened to kill Vicente for his disrespect.

At this tense moment, Pizarro ordered the attack. The cannons fired, and the Spanish charged from their positions. It is often stated in modern studies of the event that Atahualpa's retinue was completely unarmed, as a sign of good faith. While it was a diplomatic procession, this assertion is not fully true – they carried knives, lassos, and ceremonial axes, on top of outnumbering the concealed Spaniards 45:1.[11] Had they tried to overwhelm the Spanish, the effort would have likely been successful, and the ambush stymied.

However, the Spanish had made good use of their mystique among the Inca. Until this point, cannon and harquebus usage had been limited in order to conserve supplies – but here the Spanish unleashed an overwhelming volley from all sides. Though their firearms were limited in number, the sudden noise and smoke terrified the Incan nobles. The conquistadors had also affixed bells to their saddles for added noise and psychological impact. This made their initial cavalry charge louder and more imposing.

The resulting scene was pure chaos. Atahualpa's retinue scattered, falling everywhere to Spanish blades and shot. In an effort to escape, a portion of the crowd trampled Cajamarca's walls, fleeing toward the soldiers encamped outside. Apparently terrified, this portion of Atahualpa's army fled as well.

In the town, the Spanish killed or took prisoner most of those who remained. During the initial chaos, Spanish soldiers pushed through the crowd to Atahualpa, cutting his carriers down and pulling him from his litter. Pizarro, in the thick of the fighting, charged toward the king. Just as a Spanish infantryman was about to kill the Incan king, Pizarro stopped the man's sword with his hand. The resulting wound was the only casualty sustained by the Spanish.

Wildly outnumbered and trapped in enemy territory, they had effectively conquered the Incan empire in one daring move. It was an act that would look at home if listed as an exploit of Odysseus.

~

Pizarro's mistake came in the months and years that followed this conquest. After meeting no resistance on the trek to Cuzco… Pizarro *stopped*.

This man, clearly destined for a full life of exploration and combat, instead settled into governorship of Peru. He became bogged down in politics, rather than continually pushing the frontier forward. As a result, he spent his later years engaged in debate and intra-Spanish strife, namely with his former ally Almagro.

When he won this conflict in 1538 and executed Almagro, Pizarro effectively signed his death warrant. Only three years later, armed supporters of the other conquistador would burst into his home, attacking his family and guests, intent on replacing him as governor.

Pizarro, 63 at the time, put up an admirable resistance – killing two attackers and wounding a third. He was finally defeated only when "he became too exhausted to brandish his sword."[12] The conqueror of Peru's last act was to draw a cross on the ground – in his own blood – and kiss it.

COLUMBUS

And so we return to Columbus, discoverer of the New World and initiator of all the conquests of these other great men. Here, I would like to discuss an alternative view of Columbus, something that hints at a greater sense of genius than even the pre-Zinn description of his voyage.

That is: the idea that Columbus knew from the beginning where he was going.

This view stands in stark contrast to the commonly-accepted story of Columbus, which (moralizing and propaganda aside) asserts that he aimed to find a passage to Asia via travelling west. This route was based on Columbus' own geographical calculations, which cut the diameter of Earth nearly in half. The orthodoxy surrounding Columbus also maintains that he never admitted to discovering something other than Asia, and went to his grave insisting that he had landed on an outlying island of China or India.

But there is a compelling case to be made for the idea that he did not, in fact, set off in 1492 for an Asian trade route; that his proposal was intentionally and obviously farcical, meant to conceal his true knowledge.

Prior to his voyage across the Atlantic, Columbus had undertaken numerous trade voyages both north and south of Iberia. While sailing for Portugal – the preeminent navigational power of the early Age of Exploration, and notoriously guarded with their knowledge of trade winds, ports, and currents – he had learned the best navigational techniques of his day, studying maps and charts that were usually kept secret from foreigners. He had also worked as a bookseller, and despite not being a scholar by trade, was extraordinarily well-read and educated.

All of this is accepted historical truth. The traditional narrative goes on to say that Columbus had read heavily on the known geography of the Atlantic, namely *Imago Mundi*, a work by the French scholar Pierre d'Ailly which argued that the ocean wasn't nearly as large as was assumed. In the margins of Columbus' copy (which is preserved today), he had written: "There is no reason to believe that the ocean covers half the world."[13] In support of this hypothesis, he consulted maps new and old, and found inconsistencies which could support the idea that Earth was half its accepted size. This new geography would make the east coast of Asia just *barely* reachable in a journey of a month or so, with stops at its easternmost islands for supplies.

He then proposed this hypothesis to the King John II of Portugal – whose court scholars laughed him out almost immediately. They called his proposal a death-wish, his scholarship fanciful and absurd. Columbus had long been a reputable sailor and navigator, but they saw this proposal as a lapse in judgement, or perhaps a bout of madness.

When he took the idea to Spain, Ferdinand and Isabella's court scholars came to similar conclusions. However, they were at least slightly more open to the concept. Perhaps their court entertained this idea more seriously due to weaker maritime knowledge, or a willingness to accept radical ideas that could disrupt Portuguese naval dominance. Either way, they at least gave Columbus an audience. Even then, six years of talks consistently ended in stalemate, with only fringe elements of the Spanish court supporting Columbus.

Frustrated, he threatened to take the proposal to France, leaving in a rage. While riding out of Spain on a donkey, he was recalled and the voyage was finally funded – likely based on the calculation that an embarrassment by France (in the case of Columbus' success) would outweigh the financial outlay of supporting his probable suicide mission. And so, Columbus set off across the Atlantic, aiming for Asia.

This story, taken at face value, makes absolutely no sense.

By the late fifteenth century, scholars knew well the size of the Earth, with astonishing accuracy given their technology. In fact, the first approximate calculation of the Earth's circumference had been done by Eratosthenes – over a century before the birth of Christ![14] Even when his work was lost in the West, monks during Late Antiquity and the Middle Ages had completed and verified similar calculations, based on astronomical observations; additionally, Muslim scholars had come to similar conclusions during the Islamic Golden Age.

All of these calculations were widely available to scholars in Portugal and Spain, and well-known among the court astronomers and cartographers who rejected Columbus' premise. It was instantly and obviously absurd to anyone with a serious education.

Traditionally, this absurdity is explained by asserting that Columbus just "wasn't that good" at math or cartography. Considering his lifetime of naval success and career as a cartographer, as well as his impressive navigation across the Atlantic, this is a weak explanation. At best, it is hand-waving to fill gaps in the historical record. The alternative explanation requires some context as to the politics surrounding naval exploration in the late 1400s.

The Age of Exploration had begun only a few decades prior, pioneered by Henry the Navigator beginning in 1418 but only reaching prominence by the 1450s. At the time of Columbus' voyage, the Portuguese were focusing most of their energies on navigating increasingly along the African coast, seeking a sea route to Asia in order to circumvent Ottoman control of the Silk Road. Spain, France, and England were desperately trying to catch up, funding similar expeditions and investing in naval technology to varying degrees.

The culture among sailors for each nation, particularly in Portugal and Spain, was thus one of entrepreneurial spirit, national pride, and ruthless competition. Naval exploration was dangerous and expensive, but incredibly lucrative; each expedition funded by the crown functioned something like a modern startup. Each proposed voyage was a venture seeking millions in investment, for a high-risk endeavor with a potentially massive upside.

In this unpredictable environment, inside knowledge and personal reputation reigned supreme. Astronomical charts, trade winds, currents: these were industry secrets, and important matters of personal and national security. Many discoveries were kept under lock and key, or only shared by word of mouth. Personal recommendations meant everything. The entire culture of captains, court scholars, and royal investors was thus one of high trust and extreme concern. Imagine a group of modern venture capitalists, their analysts in tow, considering the latest proposal of someone who's had a dozen successful startups and exits; this was the situation between Columbus at the Portuguese, then Spanish, royal court.

It was in this environment that Columbus made his proposal, which was immediately recognized as ridiculous. His claims about the size of the Earth were demonstrably false; and, even if they were true, the distance of the voyage stretched the limits of publicly-known sailing techniques.

On top of this, Columbus asked for laughably generous terms. Namely, he requested a 10% share of all ongoing trade along his route, as well as governorship of any lands conquered in the voyage. By contemporary standards, this was a *massive* ask. If he truly did find a route to China, trade with the East would immediately dominate the Spanish economy, and other European powers would begin using the same route, unencumbered by such a massive cut given to the discoverer.

Additionally, the idea that Columbus would conquer lands in East Asia was bold, to say the least. From the writings of Marco Polo and dozens of other sources, scholar of Columbus' day (and Columbus himself) knew that East Asia was controlled by vast, powerful empires, none of which he could conquer with a few lightly-armed men, thousands of miles from support.

So, in total: Columbus' math was drastically wrong, his terms were absurd given the stated goals of the voyage, and these goals made very little sense in context. What are investors meant to conclude from this?

That Columbus *knew something* he wasn't letting on.

His proposal was *intentionally* ludicrous.[15] Columbus was not a person prone to rash reasoning or sloppy thinking, and his recommendations said as much. These letters were high accolades from prior investors and associates, an introduction which gave him an audience at the Spanish royal court. They knew he was competent. So, the intended inference was that he presented this farcical theory to conceal something only he knew – some inside edge he couldn't publicize.

If Columbus had openly stated that his goals were to discover and conquer an unknown continent across the Atlantic, the risk of another group setting off first would be too great. Again, navigation at this time was dominated by secrecy and intense competition. He couldn't risk losing that edge to a competitor.

But where did Columbus get this idea? What actually *was* his insider information?

This is where we see a deeper genius in Columbus, and get a better sense of the brazen courage involved in his voyage across the Atlantic. His pieces of evidence for the New World, when taken alone, were little more than legends and rumors. But, when taken in combination and approached with rigor, they provide a more comprehensive image of his voyage as a highly *intentional* act, based on rumors and legends carefully examined and combined into a groundbreaking revelation.

First of all, as a Portuguese sailor and captain, Columbus would have certainly known about the rumors of lands to the west. Numerous Portuguese captains had made unsuccessful voyages deep into the Atlantic, looking for islands or perhaps continents – for example, Fernão Teles in 1475 and Fernão Dulmo in 1486.[16] These voyages were based on old legends of the island of Antilia in the western Atlantic – as well as rumored sightings of land in the region, by Portuguese captains heading toward the Cape of Good Hope.

When travelling south, sailing ships had to swing west from the coast of Africa, as trade winds there were more favorable than those along the coast of Africa; for decades, numerous historians have argued that Portuguese ships, blown too far west of this path, were likely the first to sight the outlying islands of the Americas. However, these expeditions probably never landed – or, if they landed, did not survive the return trip. This argument was recently bolstered by the uncovering of a Portuguese nautical chart dated to 1424, which shows Antilia as an island in the western Atlantic, at a corresponding location to the vanguard islands of the New World, or perhaps even the easternmost reaches of Brazil.[17] This charted landmass lacks detail (it is simply recorded as a square island), suggesting that it was merely sighted but not explored. While this era was driven by men who felt a call toward new frontiers, it was still heavily based around commerce; such an unplanned landing would be extremely risky for a merchant vessel, a fact which could explain the lack of investigation. The critical point, though, is that Portuguese sailors knew of *something* across the Atlantic – even if they hadn't yet explored it. Columbus would have almost certainly been privy to these rumors, as well as maps which charted the presence of untouched lands in the western Atlantic.

But this is not all: consider also the Viking settlement of Greenland and North America, undertaken and abandoned centuries prior to the Age of Exploration. This act was not known by scholars at the time, but it *had* been recorded in legends and rumors among Nordic seaside towns.[18] This is a notion that Columbus, as a navigator and heavy reader, would have likely been interested in – and something he would have had access to during his time in Iceland or other northern ports. Similar tales existed in the annals of Irish cultural history: for example, stories of the monk Saint Brendan, who had allegedly travelled to modern-day Canada on a leather-skinned ship.[19]

Again: myths, legends, rumors. Vague notions of *something* being out there, but without a clear guide. When Columbus' thinking is understood in this more complete context, his note in the margins of *Imago Mundi* takes on a decidedly different tone:

There is no reason to believe that the ocean covers half the world... Not because the Earth is half-sized, but because there's something *there!*

After coming to this opinion over years of reading and research, Columbus knew that it was the most valuable "alpha" of his era, perhaps of all time. His ridiculous proposal hinted that he was knew some piece of critical information, something so important that he refused to even reveal it. But it was information he was willing to bet his life on. The hand-wavy math, the absurd terms – these were hints that something far greater than trade with China was at stake.

Later quotations usually cited in support of the traditional theory – that Columbus died thinking he had landed in Asia – also take on a different tone when viewed in light of the secretive, competitive world of fifteenth-century exploration. For example, Columbus had the entire crew of his third voyage take an oath not to counter the interpretation that they had landed on an Asian island chain; he threatened a massive fine and the "cutting of the tongue" upon anyone who publicly said otherwise.[20] This act is often cited as proof of Columbus' megalomania, or his rigidity of belief – but does it not seem more like a futile attempt to keep his discovery of the New World a secret?

Other sources cited in support of the traditional framework should also be called into question by Columbus' extreme penchant for secrecy. On the initial voyage, he kept separate captain's logs, one to appease his fearful crew and one for private use. He wrote his journal entries in Greek, maintaining one for submission to the Spanish crown and one for personal writing. Even his signature was a cipher, with an unclear meaning that still draws debate today. Taking this into account, should we not survey his actions more closely for potentially layered meanings? The subtext of his request to the Spanish court certainly suggests a deeper level of thinking than its stated explanations, and should call into question the interpretation of other, later acts.

It is also worth noting that Columbus' "new model" of the world placed the eastern coast of Asia at almost exactly the same place as the east coast of the Americas – quite the coincidence, considering that there are only two true east coasts in the world. Whether by rumor, now-lost texts, or secret maps, Columbus had concluded that a landmass existed *and* derived its approximate location. With his navigational knowledge and some careful planning, he had also solved how to get there and return safely, using trade winds and the currents of the North Atlantic gyre.

Even with this knowledge, the trip across the Atlantic was completely conjectural, a bet with the equivalent of millions of dollars and hundreds of men's lives – Columbus' included. It was an *incredibly* risky enterprise, the contemporary equivalent to the moon landing. The math had been worked out, and the technology tested… but the execution was still a massive risk. It would require shrewd leadership, which Columbus certainly provided in the arduous journey.

Columbus' management of the newly-discovered territory is divisive today, but this shrewd leadership and visionary daring cannot be denied. Everyone who heard of the voyage told him it was suicidal, impossible; even the crew had second thoughts midway through, threatening a mutiny. But he never faltered in his dedication to pushing the boundaries of what was possible. In that sense Columbus was a true frontiersman, venturing into the unknown with lofty goals and no way home.

And, perhaps, a sense of genius that has gone unappreciated for far too long.

IV

A New Approach to the Age of Exploration

Clearly, a new perspective on the Age of Exploration is long overdue. Instead of viewing the age with scolding condemnation, we must focus on the deeds of the men who defined the era: Columbus, the risk-taker and frontiersman; Cortés, the brilliant tactician and orator; Pizarro, the indefatigable warrior and bold trickster; and many others of equal daring and willpower.

All were men out of their time, imbued with a more ancient drive for conquest. And yet – all pious Christians, who strove to improve upon the lands and peoples they had attained in battle.

The deeply Christian morality of these men is an element of the debate which I have touched on so far, but one that certainly requires more attention. In my profiles of the conquistadors, I focused primarily on their military prowess, the shrewdness and ambition of their campaigns, because I believe that these are the traits for which they should be primarily remembered. The conquistadors should be regarded as similar figures to Alexander, Caesar, and Napoleon – beacons of inspiration and greatness. Men who took great risks and prevailed against impossible odds. Men of faith and will.

But of course, the debate over the Age of Exploration is often concerned less with this element and more with the well-being of the conquered peoples, largely due to Zinn's focus on studying history only in order to understand "the plight of the downtrodden." So, it is worth dedicating a few words to the truth about Spanish colonial rule in the New World.

Today, the lifestyle of conquered natives in Spanish colonies is often reduced to pure oppression, the worst and largest-scale slavery the world has ever seen; the lies about Columbus' frenzy for chopped-off hands and constant rape are taken as fact, and as representative of all Spanish government in the New World. This reframe was the original version of the *1619 Project*, an attempt at polluting the founding mythos of the Americas by claiming it was uniquely and horribly defined by slavery, and that no one may ever be free of that legacy.

But, frankly, this "legacy" is vastly overblown and chronically misused.

The encomienda system in particular is highlighted as a racist endeavor, something unique to European colonies in the Americas and unmatched by any other cruelty in history. In reality, the encomienda system was merely an expansion of Spanish feudal policies in the Old World, and resembled the typical labor systems of the era across the world. In fact, the encomienda system was carried over from Spain, where it was used to reward participants in the Reconquista with land and labor in a feudal arrangement. Thus, as vassals of the Spanish crown, conquered natives lived essentially as peasants did in Europe, or practically anywhere else. They were required to pay tribute to lords, and required to work in specific farming areas. Most direct administration and organization was actually undertaken by native leaders, as encomienda were typically granted to only one man or family, and it was easiest to simply adapt existing social structures to the new governmental system. Additionally, while encomienda owners were due tribute from natives, they were also required to arrange for education, protection, and the building of infrastructure, in a sort of formalized *noblesse oblige*. Many today will sneer at this obligation, pretending that it was never fulfilled – but the rapid adoption of the Spanish language and Catholic faith in the region tells a different story.

With this said – abuses by Spaniards absolutely occurred, especially when the Spanish New World was nascent and less-regulated. Most commonly, encomienda holders did not properly pay subjects for their labor, and forced natives on long expeditions for pearl-fishing. However, these abuses were actively prosecuted by the Spanish crown, and by no means the expectation of the system or the norm. Additionally, these abuses are exaggerated in the historical record due to contemporary propaganda from other European powers, particularly the Protestant nations of northern Europe (which aimed to paint Spanish Catholics as backwards and oppressive on purely religious and political grounds). The sensational claims of Dutch and English writers about Spanish atrocities are repeated uncritically today, as proof of widespread abuses in the New World; this is known in historiography as the Spanish Black Legend, and widely accepted to be sensationalized and untrue.[21] For more details on the Black Legend, the writings of historians Philip Wayne Powell and Richard Kagan are instructive.

Historical propaganda aside, it is worth noting that the abuses which did actually happen were addressed with a massive policy change in 1542: the *New Laws of the Indies for the Good Treatment and Preservation of the Indians*, signed by Charles V.[22] The system established by the New Laws replaced the encomienda hierarchy and abolished true slavery in Spanish holdings – an act which actually gave Amerindian vassals *more rights* than their Spanish-governed counterparts in Europe.

Additionally, criticism of Spanish rule in the New World often conveniently overlooks what the previous system looked like. The Aztecs demanded hundreds or even thousands of human sacrifices each year from their subjects – on top of requiring tribute labor, slaves, and taxes. The word "extractive" is often applied to European colonies – yet this Aztec system of rule is simply seen as "how things were." Similarly, Incan society was based on tribute labor and slavery, often far more brutal than anything the worst of the Spanish could have ever undertaken – simply due to the massive size and broad geographic presence of Incan armies, as compared to the relatively few Spaniards in the New World.

Like other slanted historical interpretations, the demonization of New World colonists relies on hypocritical moral standards and cherry-picking. The vast and brutal conquests undertaken by the Aztecs are excused; in fact, their complexity, military strength, and bloodlust are lauded for some odd reason. The fact that Cortés was able to rally so many against Aztec rule is painted as some dishonest scheme, when in reality the Tlaxcala natives despised the Aztecs, and simply did not want to live under such a brutal yoke anymore. Similarly, the Inca are described exclusively with glowing praise, as a wonderful and advanced civilization. Dishonest historians ignore their bloody conquests and their total war practices, as well as their practice of Qhapaq Hucha (ritual child sacrifice).[23]

At the same time, the incursion of the Spanish into this supposedly Edenic paradise is demonized to no end. Their conquests were depraved and dishonest; their policies were the worst the world had ever seen; their religion was inhumane and oppressive. Modern moral rules are applied only to European conquerors – never to those who had conquered the same lands, over and over, for centuries prior. This sense of morality requires ignoring that the Spanish brought incredible infrastructure and technology to the New World; that, via missionaries and schools, they converted and educated millions; and that their system of government was far more restrained and beneficial than the ones they replaced, largely due to their Christianity. It is a weak and hypocritical sense of morality, in which rules exist only for one group, and only for the purpose of condemning their ever act and slandering their greatest heroes. It is, at its core, a malicious double standard.

This double standard reveals the true motivations behind this brand of subversion: hatred of *winners*. Simple resentment held against those who ultimately succeeded. All attacks on the Age of Exploration are derived from this founding impulse of Marxism, manifesting in historical discourse as the reductive dichotomy between evil oppressors and the pure-hearted oppressed.

Like every other element of leftist historical subversion, the demonization of the Age of Exploration is derived from a simple grudge against Western civilization, a grudge held due to backwards politics and simple racial or religious resentment.

If you accept this frame – that everything created or done by Westerners is tainted by a uniquely bad type of sin – you can never draw any inspiration from history. This is an intentional element; the shaming is by design. Everything in leftist historical discourse is aimed at scolding, at beating-down, at humiliating the reader for their beliefs or heritage. Like the concept of the "dark ages", the framing of the Age of Exploration as evil (and America's founding as some sort of original sin) is simply meant to attach shame to Western ancestry and culture. It is pure propaganda – and factually weak propaganda at that.

But in order to step over this destructive rhetoric, we must have a constructive alternative. We must draw inspiration, even pride from the men who tamed the New World. The Americas were founded not by some comical villains, but by courageous and bold men. The conquistadors should be regarded as similar figures to Alexander, Caesar, and Napoleon – beacons of inspiration and greatness. Men who took great risks and prevailed against impossible odds. Men of faith and will. America was discovered and conquered by men who held this Will to Power, a Faustian drive to explore and tame new frontiers.

And, once their military conquests were secured, these men did not merely extract tribute. They built great works of civilization – cities in which millions still live today. Their strong Christian beliefs led them to convert millions, an act which should see their names inscribed in Christian history as heroes.

Additionally, the morality offered by their Christianity led them to a unique type of rule, one which actually *reigned in* the worst excesses of conquest – which in a different time or place would have occurred as a matter of policy. Instead, the lands they conquered were liberated from the bloody necrocracies which had dominated them for so long, and became Christian cultures of surplus and civilization.

All of these are objectively good and imitable things, and we should stop pretending otherwise.

~

The spirit of the conquistadors is particularly prescient today, as their example offers a historical precedent for dealing with problems that seem uniquely modern. The frontier spirit exhibited by these men is clearly recognizable in retrospect – but in their early lives, such a frontier seemed unreachable, or at least fading in viability.

Today, young men in particular lament the lack of frontiers, of civilizational edges where they can test themselves. This is often seen as a historical first – but Cortés and Pizarro faced exactly the same struggle. Their fathers had both made their mark on the world in frantic battles against the Moors and campaigns in Italy, both prospects which would not be available to their sons. They also could not look forward to any notable inheritance: Cortés' family had almost nothing to give, and Pizarro would never inherit his father's property due to his illegitimacy. Cortés was pushed into an unwanted legal career, and Pizarro's future looked as if it would never hold anything higher than swineherding.

For these men and thousands like them, all of this changed with the first whispers of Columbus' discovery across the Atlantic. With the discovery of the New World, the European concept of the world physically changed: suddenly becoming vaster, wilder, more enticing. In 1493 young men learned of an unknown and wild world just a month away by sail; a land not yet tamed, not yet owned. Ambitious young men clamored for the chance to make the voyage; to struggle against whatever hardship may come on a true frontier.

And they succeeded in grand fashion. Cortés' rebuttal to Charles V, of having claimed "more provinces than your ancestors left you cities," captures well the sheer scale of their enterprise.

The spirit which animated these men still exists today, but it languishes in individuals who lack such a frontier. Nietzsche identified the problem over a century ago: just as young men are ready to be "sent into the desert" is precisely when they are shackled by quagmirical bureaucracies – their desire for a frontier subverted into domesticity, complexity, control.[24] Since then, the frontier has only further dwindled, and today the spirit of conquest and exploration seems unreachable.

But is this not the same situation that faced Cortés, Pizarro, De Soto, and Balboa? Until 1493, the entire world – as far as they knew – was already discovered and owned. Their opportunities seemed limited, and the concept of proving themselves on a frontier probably looked laughable. Their future seemed to lay in bureaucracy or simple toil. But Columbus' discovery turned this notion on its head, changing the very shape of the world in the European (and particularly Spanish) mind. Suddenly, the tamed world of Iberia was small and inconsequential compared to the vast lands that lay across the Atlantic.

When activists smear the "gold-lust" of the conquistadors, it is because they cannot understand this innate drive to venture into unknown worlds. To dare, to conquer.

The only question that remains is this: what frontier will be discovered next? Where, or rather how, will the Pizarros of the twenty-first century test themselves beyond the edge of managerial society? Is the next frontier perhaps organizational, located in the less-regulated worlds of decentralization, cryptocurrency, AI? Or will there be a physical frontier in our lifetimes, some aspect of earth (or beyond) to tame and conquer?

Who will be our Columbus – or has he already come?

Endnotes

1. Capps, Kriston. "Why Are There Still 149 Statues of Christopher Columbus in the U.S." *Bloomberg*, 9 October 2021. Web.
2. Zinn, Howard (1980). *A People's History of the United States*.
3. Grabar, Mary (2019). *Debunking Howard Zinn: Exposing the Fake History That Turned a Generation Against America*.
4. Morison, Samuel Eliot (1970). *Admiral of the Ocean Sea: A Life of Christopher Columbus*.
5. Koning, Hans (1976). *Columbus: His Enterprise – Exploding the Myth*. Quoted in Grabar ch. 1.
6. de las Casas, Bartholomé (1552). *A Brief Account of the Destruction of the Indies*. Quoted in Grabar ch. 1.
7. Ibid. Book 1, ch. 93.
8. Díaz, Bernal, tr. by Lockhart, John Ingram (1844). *The Memoirs of the Conquistador Bernal Diaz del Castillo, Written by Himself, Containing a True and Full Account of the Discovery and Conquest of Mexico and New Spain*.
9. Folsom, George (1843). *The Dispatches of Hernando Cortés, the Conqueror of Mexico, addressed to the Emperor Charles the Fifth, Written During the Conquest, and Containing a Narrative of its Events*.
10. Prescott, W. H. (2011). *The History of the Conquest of Peru*.
11. Hemming, John (1987). *The Conquest of the Incas*.
12. Stirling, Stuart (2005). *Pizarro: Conqueror of the Inca*.
13. Weiner, Eric. "Coming to America: Who Was First?" *NPR*, 8 October 2007. Web.
14. *Eratosthenes and the Circumference of the Earth*. *Nature* **152**, 473 (1943).
15. The theory of Columbus having deduced the existence of the New World has been approached by numerous thinkers, but this specific framework was first proposed by The American Sun in 2022 [www.theamericansun.com].
16. Josephy Jr., Alvin M. "Was America Discovered Before Columbus?" *American Heritage*, April 1955, Vol. 6 Issue 3. Accessed online.
17. Ibid.
18. Linden, Eugene. "The Vikings: A Memorable Visit to America". *Smithsonian Magazine*, December 2004. Web.
19. Carberry, Seán. "Did St. Brendan arrive in America before Christopher Columbus?" *Irish Central*, 9 October 2022. References *Navigatio*.
20. "The Second and Third Voyages of Christopher Columbus". *Encyclopedia Britannica*. Web.
21. Jones, Sam. "Spain Fights to Dispel Legend of Inquisition and Imperial Atrocities". *The Guardian*, 29 April 2018. Web.

22. "New Laws of the Indies for the Good Treatment and Preservation of the Indians, 1542". *North Carolina State University college of Humanities and Social Sciences.* Web.
23. Cockrell, Brian. "Capac Hucha as an Incan Assemblage". *Art of the Ancient Americas, Department of the arts of Africa, Oceania, and the Americas, the Metropolitan Museum of Art*, November 2017. Web.
24. Nietzsche, Friedrich (1881). *Dawn of Day.* 178.

About the Author:

Alaric the Barbarian is the founder and editor of The Dissident Review. Aside from that, most other records have been lost to history.

Follow him on Twitter: @0xAlaric

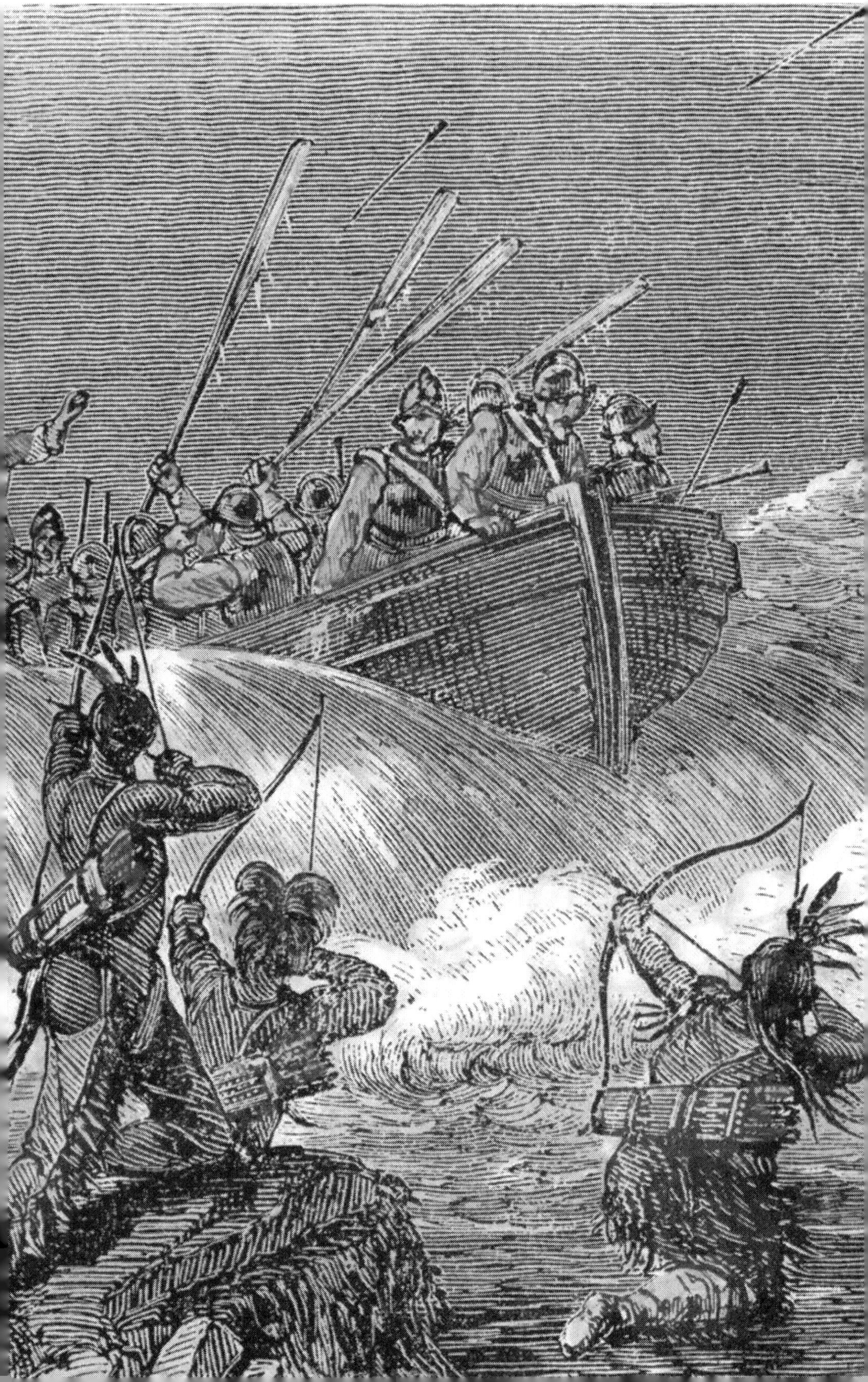

The Inevitability of Conquest

By Peter Iversen

> *War is nothing but a duel on a larger scale. Countless duels go to make up a war, but a picture of it as a whole can be formed by imagining a pair of wrestlers. Each tries through physical force to compel the other to do his will; his immediate aim is to throw his opponent in order to make him incapable of further resistance. War is thus an act of force to compel our enemy to do our will…and there is no logical limit to the application of that force. Each side, therefore, compels its opponent to follow suit; a reciprocal action is started which must lead, in theory, to extremes.*
>
> —Carl von Clausewitz, *On War*

The arrival of the Europeans to the New World sparked a clash of civilizations that, at first blush, one would imagine would end with the swift defeat of the native Amerindians, none of whom had passed the Bronze Age. The conflict, however, fulminated for hundreds of years — in the United States, the last of the Indian Wars ended with the Apache Wars in 1924, though some believe that rogue warbands still lurk in the Sierra Madre mountains. The Amerindians were finally conquered and absorbed into the American Empire, but as the Empire enters its final decline and the ability of the central government to control the individual state governments wanes, the Amerindians and the other dissident minorities of the American Moderns have begun to reassert their separateness.

The new historiography represented by such progressive historians as Howard Zinn, Nikole Hannah-Jones, and Dee Brown has reinterpreted this conflict as the illegitimate conquest of an innocent, indigenous people by a treacherous, foreign invader. The question of legitimacy is a difficult one to answer, not only because the ethics of war are the *ad hoc* justification of a uniquely Atlanticist world order, but also because what the Europeans believed was proper in war was different from what the Amerindians believed, and what the Amerindians believed was proper changed as they transitioned from being prehistoric to historic to modern peoples. How, then, should we think of the men who represent the European conquest of the New World: Christopher Columbus, the Pilgrims, George Armstrong Custer, or many others?

To give just one example, Lt. Col. Custer led the US Army 7th Cavalry in a raid of the Southern Cheyenne winter encampment at Washita River in 1868, killing somewhere between 13 and 150, including anywhere between "some" and 75 women and children, and capturing a further 53 women and children. Contemporary journalists and the Cheyenne themselves view the Battle as a massacre, and modern historians argue over many aspects: what defines a massacre; were those Southern Cheyenne innocent bystanders; and even if Custer had ordered the slaying of non-combatants. The answers to these questions depend critically on how we understand the nature of war and if there can be such a thing as a "just war".

The question of how to wage the illusive "just war" is intertwined with the ways that war *has* been carried out. Modern observers in the Atlanticist tradition of "rules-based order" and the "Westphalian State system" claim to obey the prescriptions of the Just War tradition expounded by thinkers like Michael Walzer, but work to reinforce the status quo in which the world is subordinated to the whims and demands of the United States as "global policeman". Who determines if a given conflict is a "just war"? Who determines the "responsibility to protect"? Who determines legitimate and illegitimate? Ask an Iraqi, Libyan, Afghani, Serb, or Syrian how they feel about the "protection" they received from the United States and its allies. Such a system can only function for so long as its members and subordinates believe that they can rely on it to satisfy their grievances. Without that, they have no reason to respect it or its rules.

The Just War Tradition demands a just cause, which most often takes the form of a response to aggression from a foreign nation, or as a preventative action against future aggression. However, this structure means that all wars can be justified as long as they are sufficiently argued. The current Russian-Ukraine war is the result of decades of rising tension, forcing us to ask who is given the right to declare a just war. An aggressor—the active agent—will always be motivated to claim justification, and the defender—the passive agent—will always be motivated to deny it. Russia invaded Ukraine with the explicitly stated purpose of protecting the Russophone minority in Ukraine, especially in the breakaway oblasts of Donetsk and Luhansk. Ukraine has an interest—a stark material interest—in denying the allegations of oppression and that the rebellious oblasts have any legitimate right to separate from Ukraine. The United States and its NATO allies which have their own geopolitical interest in an independent Ukraine, have roundly denied Russian justifications.

War as Clausewitz describes it is merely politics by another means—the resolution to competition for resources. People require resources—food, water, land—to live, and as people naturally increase, those needs will also naturally increase. Nations rely, like the people they contain, on the *lebensraum* they encompass. Just as trees compete for access to sunlight, and tall trees block the light from reaching the forest floor, so too will states compete. After all, men need to eat, and when food is limited, the man who gives will always be conquered by a man who takes. Taking is not good *per se*, but survival is good because life is good, and death is bad. As Carl Schmitt tells us, all men have an instinctive understanding of the distinction between friend and enemy, leading us to the conclusion that to give to a friend is good, while to take from an enemy is not bad.

The ancient Israelites spoke of war against *hamas*, violence that was a rebellion against God's order, threatening to upend the order of creation. Their answer was clear: they must not be allowed to live, lest they lead the faithful to sin and incur God's wrath. It is not the Israelites who go to war, then, but the enemy who has declared war on God's plan for humanity and the duty of the Israelites to defend it. It is their holy obligation to chastise the people who rebel. This sense of war was common among the kingdoms of the ancient world—the Mesopotamian kings went to war to establish order in the world just as their god, Marduk, did. The Egyptian Pharoah was a holy entity who led the forces of order against chaos, so by definition, his wars were good and just. The insistence that their wars were defensive is mirrored in other traditions: the Romans, Egyptians, Hittites, and Assyrians were all prone to claiming that their many wars were purely defensive, even when those wars were preventive wars to prevent future hostility. In stark contrast, semi-nomadic tribes viewed war and looting as good in and of itself, bringing glory to the warriors. The Amerindians largely followed this latter tradition, which they applied to their practice of scalping, horse rustling, and "counting coup", the practice of touching an enemy and leaving unharmed.

Some of this lives on in the Just War tradition, most obviously the reification of the defensive war, though just as the Romans made alliances specifically to justify them going to war, so too do modern states create the conditions that justify their wars. NATO has only expanded since the fall of the Soviet Union, and it was the proposed induction of Ukraine into NATO—Russia's final red line—that compelled the Russians to their final act of aggression. Who caused the Russian-Ukraine war? Is it the provoking NATO, incrementally hemming in through sanctions and espionage, or Russia, who actually put tanks on the ground? It is only the arrogance and folly of the West that believes that aggression must be violence, gunpowder, and plastic explosives. A mother is no less grieved at the death of her son whether he was killed by a bullet or hunger.

Let us return to the question of the Europeans and the Amerindians. The peopling of the New World followed the retreat of the glaciers across a virgin landscape. The first people, the Pioneer Foragers, were small bands of kin, wandering a land nearly devoid of people. On the rare occasions that they did meet another, they must have fought—we know that even chimpanzees will go to war over hunting grounds—but it is likely that skirmishes were rare and killing even more so. Once the population had grown enough that bands regularly clashed, they restricted themselves—or were forcibly restricted—to home ranges. As populations continued to grow, they were forced to find new sources of food, such as plant cultivation or bison, or take them from someone who did.

Three thousand years ago on the Great Plains, the Amerindians first learned proper agriculture, pottery, and the art of burying the dead in earthen mounds. One thousand years ago, the first tribes appeared in large, defended villages while the Cahokia chiefdom sprang up near St. Louis, Missouri and the Oneota culture emerged along the upper Mississippi River and Apple River. It was the establishment of settled agricultural centers that created the conditions of war: wealthy settlements with abundant stores of food and hungry bands in the hinterlands. During the years of drought, these raids would have been especially prevalent. During the hundreds of years that passed between the rise of tribes along the Mississippi River and the entry of Europeans into the New World, we know that the Oneota grew from their homeland in Wisconsin and Minnesota to expel the inhabitants of Cahokia from southern Illinois and pushed the people of the Central Plains out of Kansas, Nebraska, Iowa, and Missouri into South Dakota along the

Missouri River. The largest prehistoric massacre site known among the Amerindians, at Crow Creek in South Dakota, occurred when the village was repairing its defensive walls. The village, already harangued by the Oneota, was ultimately extirpated by them: at least 486 individuals, almost all of whom were scalped, and the women and children carried away.

Lewis Binford, the father of modern archaeology, wrote his magnum opus, *Constructing Frames of Reference*, as a synthesis of the hundreds of hunter-gatherer groups around the globe in an attempt to understand how the interaction between man and habitat influences culture. One major conclusion is that the forces that compelled disparate kinship bands to coalesce into tribes, and finally into chiefdoms, result from population density and the competition for resources. As foraging bands begin to encroach on each other's hunting grounds, they naturally restrict themselves to home ranges. In order to make up for the resulting loss in resources, they turn to new food sources, learning cultivation, domestication, and aquaculture. As they continue to expand, neighboring tribes will either merge or go to war. We might imagine that this explains why chiefdoms go to war, eventually resulting in the formation of empires, either as the confederation of individual chiefdoms or the subjugation of neighboring chiefdoms. This is the pattern that the Mayans, Aztecs, and Incans followed, and it is the pattern that *may* have been followed by the Cahokian culture, the Oneota culture, the Ancestral Pueblo, or the Iroquois had the Europeans not arrived in the New World. As it is, the Iroquois remained enormously powerful even after the arrival of the Europeans and it was not until their involvement in the American Revolution that the Iroquois League was split.

The arrival of the Europeans marked the inevitability of the decline and dispossession of the Amerindians. There are two closely related points: (1) even without the arrival of Europeans, one of the large agricultural Amerindian powers would have evolved to be an imperial power and conquered much of North America, akin to Alexander the Great; and (2) once the

Europeans arrived in the New World, the industrialization and continuous population growth of the European colonies would have necessarily pushed the Amerindians west. The North American Amerindians were chalcolithic peoples, and the Incans were nascent Bronze Age peoples, so by analogy with Eurasian history, we can estimate that a conquering empire would have arisen in South America in 4000 AD, and in North America in 5000 AD. By contrast, the Eurasian chalcolithic age began in 5000 BC, the Bronze Age began in 3000 BC, and the Iron Age around 1000 BC. The massive Persian Empire reached its peak in size around 500 BC before being conquered by Alexander the Great in the fourth century BC.

The Europeans had thousands of years of experience in agriculture, industry, and warfare: by the time they arrived in the New World they had cannons and guns for over one hundred years, and were experimenting with rifling which would convert the famously inaccurate musket into the American long rifle and finally the rifled muskets and repeating rifles common during the American Civil War. The Amerindians were able to obtain firearms and ammunition but lacked the capacity to produce it themselves—the same reason that the Confederacy was ultimately unable to defeat the Union in the American Civil War was that the industrialization of the North was a force multiplier that the South was unable to overcome. The swift adoption of hybrid agricultural practices by the European colonists, along with their use of draft animals, access to trade markets, and the transmission of Old-World diseases to the Amerindians helped cement the toehold in the region, but many early colonies died out or merged with local tribes. The presence of furs, lumber, and fertile land, however, proved to be irresistible to Europeans who flocked to the region. The constant influx of migrants, coupled with their rapid rate of reproduction, ensured that they would outnumber the Amerindians unless there was a unified plan among the natives to forcibly expel them at every opportunity.

War, then, was inevitable. The European and Amerindian societies could not coexist because the Europeans relied on the conversion of Native lands to colonial farms and ranches which the natives were barred from, creating an existential crisis for the Amerindians. This is what is meant by the clash of civilizations: two great cultures, alike in dignity, cannot coexist forever. What begins as insignificant tensions grow along with the populations of each into aggression and outright warfare. Was it wrong for the Europeans to conquer the Amerindians? We might as well ask if it was wrong of Alexander the Great to conquer the Persians, or if it is wrong for a lion to hunt a gazelle: it merely is. The Europeans travelled to the New World in search of *lebensraum*; we eat to live, and whether by hunting or faring, this requires land. Land held by the Europeans is land denied to the Amerindians. A farm planted by the British provides crops for the British, just as a deer hunted by the French feeds the French. Just as the Oneota wiped out the people of Crow Creek, life demands a *lebensraum*, and men will kill to obtain it.

All states, once they exceed a certain size and density, are forced to resort to conquest: the subjugation of another people by the force of arms or wit, and the conversion of their self-improvement to the benefit of the empire that they find themselves subsumed by. History is replete with tales of conquest, and there is hardly any period of history where no conquest took place. The Israelites conquered the Levant, the Romans conquered the Gauls, the Normans conquered the Saxon kingdoms of Britain, the Aztecs conquered the city-states of Mesoamerica as far as Guatemala, and the Incans conquered the Andean mountains from Ecuador to Chile. We should not, however, assume that all conquest requires violence: China is in the process of conquering many African nations *economically*, and Europe has been *culturally* conquered by an Atlanticist regime headed by the United States. Nor do all conquests relate only to resources: the American odyssey of "making the world safe for democracy", begun in World War I and continued through the Cold War, was accomplished as much through war as by diplomacy.

If we accept that wars are inevitable, then we lead ourselves to the question of how should states engage in war? The Just War theory has an answer to this question, the so-called *jus in bello*, with many stipulations: the strict distinction between combatants and noncombatants, the prohibition of acts which as "evil in themselves", *mala in se*, and the ban on reprisals. It should be obvious that these restraints can only be understood and applied in a particular context: professional armies fighting on a battlefield away from any other human being, each abiding by a strict code of honor that permits neither treachery, wrath, nor glory-seeking. In short, war waged by automatons. However, we know that warfare is motivated by glory, wealth, vengeance, loyalty, and all manner of emotions that give a sharp edge to the friend-enemy distinction. The taking of loot and warbrides, and the emptying of landscapes to open them for repopulation are *technologies* for the execution of war for the achievement of certain goals. The Amerindians took warbrides just as the ancient Eurasians did—to regenerate their tribes. They took loot for the same reason that all cultures did—warfare is costly and demands repayment. They eliminated their enemies and burnt their villages for the same reason as anyone else—to establish their *lebensraum*.

Nor is the prohibition of targeting civilians absolute, even in modern warfare. Russia has received criticism for its practice of targeting power generation facilities in Ukraine, which has the twin results of denying electrical power to the Ukrainian military, a legitimate target, and the Ukrainian populace, an illegitimate target. This must be counterbalanced, however, with the previous acts undertaken by NATO forces during the Kosovo War. At the time, Kosovo was contested between Yugoslavia and the Kosovar Albanians who had declared independence. In response to Yugoslavia's refusal to sign onto the Rambouillet Accords, which would have permanently stationed 30,000 NATO troops in Kosovo, NATO inflicted 78 days of air strikes on Yugoslavian infrastructure. The bombing campaign killed some five hundred civilians, destroyed bridges, industrial plants, hospitals, schools, and monuments in addition to Yugoslav military outposts. The destruction of the Chinese Embassy in Belgrade is the most memorable embarrassment suffered by NATO during what the US called Operation Noble Anvil. In response to accusations that the bombing campaign was depriving 70% of Yugoslav civilians access to water and power, NATO Spokesman Jamie Shea blamed Milosevic's refusal to acquiesce to NATO demands.

The rejection of these technologies of war is a self-imposed agreement between parties, to abstain from these acts so that their own peoples will be spared from the horrors of war. We must understand this, however, as sort of aristocratic restraint that acts as a prisoner's dilemma: when both sides are evenly matched, the side that fights dirty will always defeat the side that fights fair. Why, then, should any side fight fair if they cannot expect their enemy to reciprocate—if they have long and painful experience of their enemy not reciprocating? The Balkan nations have been ethnically cleansing each other's lands for nearly a century after they learned it from their experience warring to establish their nations in the collapse of the Ottoman Empire.

We want to be assured that our wars are just because we desire to be good and to be led by the good. Unfortunately, justice in war seems to be nothing more than the distinction between friend and enemy which rears its head once again: *our* wars are justified, undertaken under great deliberation and with heavy hearts; *their* wars are illegitimate attacks on innocents, carried out with reckless malice. In the end, the goodness of war is not for us to say, just as the goodness of men is not for us to say: life is good, and let God sort out the rest.

About the Author:

Pete Iversen is a writer interested in the ways that peoples and nations grow, struggle to thrive, and disappear.

Follow him on Twitter: @pete_iversen

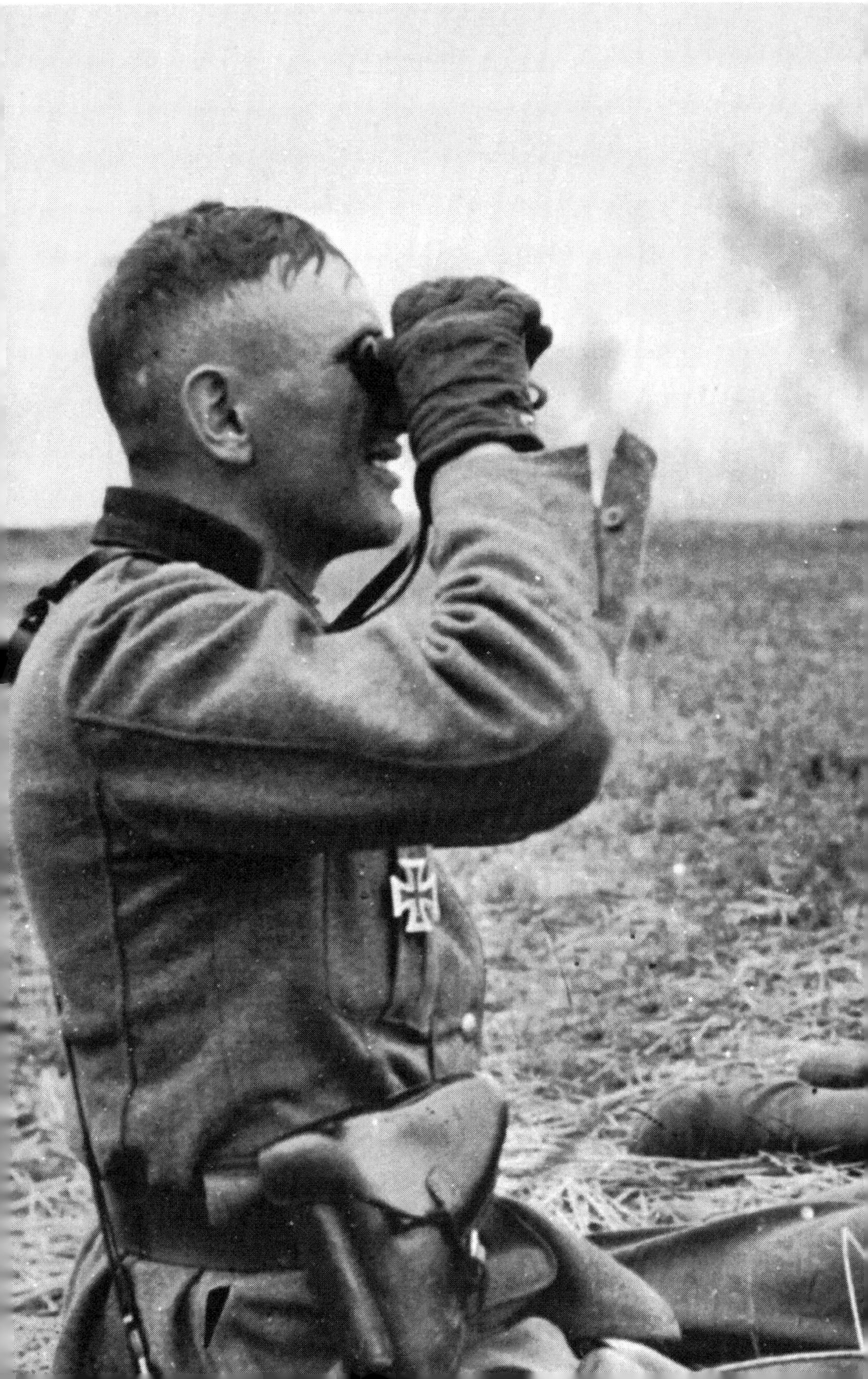

The Furthest German:

A Frontier Pushed Too Far

By Anthony Bavaria

German tank columns roll across the vast steppe of the North Caucasus region.

All invasions have a purpose, and every army a plan. One of the most common motives for war from time immemorial is the attainment of assets, whether they be in the form of land, something man-made, or natural resources. However, throughout history, there is that rare occasion—usually leading up to or right at a Spenglerian golden summit—where conquest *in and of itself* is the goal.

The reasons provided for this type of conflict are usually somewhat ephemeral—the expanding of a frontier, for the glory of an empire, living space—and these rationales are more often than not trojan horses for controlling group material gain (WWI jingoism being a good example)... but every now and then, the rhetoric actually aligns with the undertaking; it's no surprise that campaigns launched under these pretenses hold a degree of fascination unmatched at any level in the study of armed conflict: mainstream academic, popular, and dissident alike.

Sadly, the imposing visions of men that hold true to their word are paid for with the blood of subordinates. Armies can be pushed too far, to unknown ends of the earth. What goes through the minds of the common foot soldier, well beyond their frontiers and at the furthest extent of a line drawn on a map? As we will see, it is a terrifying feeling to be lost in combat, cut off from the rear, with the prospect of returning home an impossibility.

Before we examine German notions of frontier expansion and their soldiers lost at the edge of the world, it is worth noting this transient feeling has been encountered throughout martial history. Xenophon's *Anabasis* describes ten thousand Greek mercenaries fighting throughout the vast lands of Persia in the 5th century BC; though they fought for others, they were entirely Greek and after battle did not go their way, returning home was their only goal. Later, Alexander would spread Greek influence to unknown lands; the war-weariness of his phalanx is well-known by the time they reached places like modern Afghanistan, a distance of 4,000 miles on horse and foot, fighting along much of the journey. Various Roman emperors would extend their empire's borders to obscure places like modern Scotland or the edge of Mesopotamia; there are islands in the Red Sea with Roman Legion graffiti carved into rocks.[1]

Like it or not, the reasoning behind Germany's attempted conquest of the Soviet Union fits the theme of this essay well. Hitler's rationale—not to forget Western man's inalienable latent fascism—is in part one reason the Third Reich continues to hold interest with so many of the victor's descendants. I have heard the most ardent WWII enthusiasts talk about the Ostfront (often prefacing their claims with statements of allegiance to being anti-Nazi) in a way that makes it clear to all but the individual speaking on the subject that they wish the war would have turned out differently.

When one looks at Wehrmacht tasks in the East, the preposterousness of it all makes the grandiosity clear in a way that dispels any mere material gain. Yes, Nazi Germany wanted to deny Ukrainian grain and Caucasus oil to the Soviet Union while taking them for themselves, as well as to cultivate Russian soil for future German settlement, but these material gains were for an entire people, not merely a class. This was world-building as opposed to petty theft. Operation Barbarossa's planned end of hostilities, commonly known as the Arkhangelsk–Astrakhan line or simply the A-A line, was roughly 1,500 miles long and encompassed a front that would have made its defense completely impossible. This was irrelevant, because 1941's campaign was meant to be one giant knockout blow; east of the A-A line would merely be whatever remained.

As it turned out, German intelligence was massively incorrect in their estimation of Soviet manpower. Midway through Barbarossa, the Wehrmacht had captured more Red Army soldiers than they thought even existed. Once the blitzkrieg stalled, supply issues began to mount, and the first of several miserable winters commenced, the hoped-for quick victory turned into a war of attrition. Just like Alexander and name-your-Roman Emperor, Hitler had bit off more than he could chew. Had Germany sought to coordinate a dual attack on the Soviets with their Japanese ally, things may have been different, but the notion of German independence coupled with the general irrelevance of Japanese war aims in Eastern Siberia make this unrealized scenario moot. Though Barbarossa didn't make it to the A-A line—not even taking Moscow—the German Army still had plenty of fight left in them; it is interesting to consider that only until colossal war goals fell short did material consideration (mainly oil) take precedence.

Phase two of this undertaking was Case Blue: a move toward the Soviet south, specifically, the Volga River and oil-rich Caucasus region. The end goal of Blue was the oil fields of Baku, a city on the far side of the Caucasus Mountains. Known as Army Group South, the Wehrmacht made—just as in the early stages of Barbarossa—massive initial gains. Between May and July of 1942, Army Group South rolled from Eastern Ukraine to the banks of the Don River. By the end of July, the Sea of Azov was reached and the regional city of Rostov was captured. By this point in the operation, supply issues were already becoming problematic. Army Group South was split in two: Army Group B would stab east toward Stalingrad and the Volga River while Army Group A would continue south toward the Caucuses, known as Operation Edelweiss. In August, the 1st Panzer Army, the 17th Army, and the Romanian 3rd Army flooded into the vast lands of Southern Russia. By September, the German Army had reached the northern slopes of the great divider of Europe and the Middle East: the Caucasus Mountains.

Dismayed with slowing progress, Hitler took over personal command of the operation. Robert Kirchubel's *Atlas of the Eastern Front: 1941-1945* tells of "Hitler's obsession with Caucasus passes and roads,"[2] hinting at the futility of the endeavor.

German Mountain troops on what looks to be the edge of the world, surely the edge of their frontier.

This obscure corner of the war is described by Werner Haupt in *Army Group South: The Wehrmacht in Russia 1941-1945* when he states, "This area, conquered by Army Group A, was classified as being in Asia, with wide steppes and numerous intersecting rivers and brooks, few watering holes, and with scorching temperatures of 40 degrees Celsius… There were only a few settlements, for the land was populated chiefly by nomads."[3] He goes on to say: "The German soldiers entered this unknown, mysterious land with a spirit of adventure,"[4] not unlike Xenophon's men in Anatolia or Alexander's phalanx in Bactria. It's worth noting that the Russians themselves thought of this general region, specifically Kalmykia, as a no-man's land. In *Stalingrad*, author Antony Beevor writes of the Russian perspective on the place, referring to it as "the end of the world;"[5] an apt description for German men of war on the furthest extent of their briefly held frontier.

This was the second time Germanic peoples had traversed the region, the first being a large group of settlers enticed to the area by Catherine the Great as a sort of alternative option to immigration to the Americas. They came to be known as the Volga Germans, and they flourished in that river's basin for centuries, only until Stalin and eventual war; they were deported east to Siberia where millions perished—yet another genocide of Europeans largely ignored by history.

As Autumn of 1942 approached, the Germans were close to their first objective of Grozny, a regional city with massive oil production. German-trained saboteurs were airdropped into the area by the Luftwaffe with the hopes of garnering local resistance to the Soviet occupiers to clear a path for approaching Panzer columns. Further east in the vast Kalmyk Steppe, elements of the 1st Panzer Army made it to the town of Kizlyar, only 40 miles from the western shores of the Caspian Sea. Soviet command was officially terrified, since this southeastern German spearhead now threatened rail lines to Iran, where massive Western Allied war material made its way to the Eastern Front. North of Kizlyar, long-range patrols conducted by the 16th Motorized Infantry Division undertook deep reconnoiters into the steppe, and were within 20 miles of Astrakhan and had views of the Volga delta in their binoculars.[6]

Months earlier, Stalin had already issued Order no. 227, the hardline "not a step back" mandate. The penalty for unauthorized Soviet retreat was a penal colony or death. However, by this point in the operation, supply issues were now untenable for the German Army and other points of the front already began to falter, specifically in and around Stalingrad, requiring a reallocation of resources.

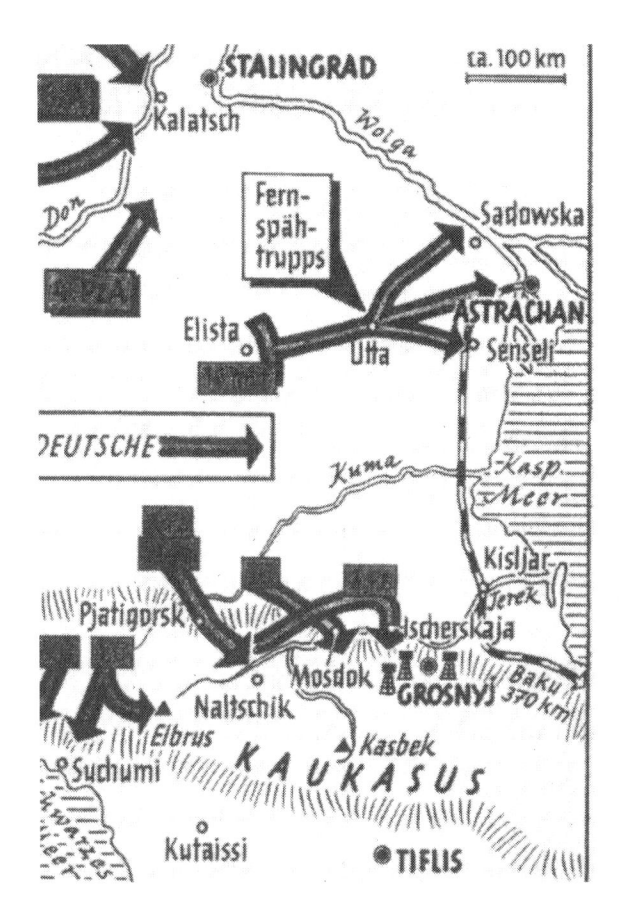

Army Group South's incursion into the southern Russian steppeland,[7] what locals referred to as "the end of the world."

Now known as Volgograd, this city is famous in the annals of Second World War history, and we all know of the Allied triumph that occurred there. The underbelly of history paints a different picture: French novelist Louis-Ferdinand Celine once infamously said, "The fall of Stalingrad is the finish of Europe."[8] Regardless, the epic battle fought there overshadows what occurred to the south. The above-mentioned town of Kizlyar and long-range patrols in the region mark the furthest advances of German troops in any direction from their Fatherland via a continuous land route—it is roughly 2,000 miles from Berlin.

These operations are the closest any German Army unit would get to the original A-A line.

What was the average Wehrmacht soldier in this far-flung corner of the globe, on the edge of the Russian steppeland, thinking at this time? Sadly, scholarship on war in the North Caucasus region is small compared to other theaters, particularly any translated to English. On the Western Front, tiny towns such as Carentan and Bastogne are lionized as the epicenters of tide-turning battles; in the East, whole regions receive a similar and often lesser treatment. The first-hand experience of German soldiers in the midst of this enterprise sadly illustrates the scope of the East as well as the futility of endless conquest.

As early as Barbarossa, in a letter to his wife, German Field Marshal von Rundstedt wrote that "the vastness of Russia devours us;"[9] exemplifying the earlier-mentioned grandiosity of Germany's eastern war aims. In *Blood Red Snow: The Memoirs of a German Soldier on the Eastern Front*, author Günter K. Koschorrek offers the fighting man's outlook. In the chapter *Fighting in Stalingrad*, he alludes to the stalling of the blitzkrieg and the end of German conquest eastward when he states, "What had happened to all the success and all the reports of the proud German Army's advances—the ones we'd heard only a few days ago? Were they exaggerations, or was this merely a temporary set-back to the usual run of successes?"[10]

As the effort to take Stalingrad crumbled, culminating in the 6th Army's encirclement, the rest of ground gained in Case Blue had to be abandoned. The capturing of oil fields or any wide-ranging goals of an A-A line or breaking into the Middle East were forever scrapped. On the question of advancing into Russia, German General Günther Blumentritt had written in his diary, "... when are we going to stop?"[11] He could have never known the halt would occur in the ancient trade crossroads of Khazaria. Beevor writes of a German company commander's experience in this vast flatland: "He began to suspect that the war had developed a momentum of its own." On Army Group A's eastern flank objective of the lower Volga, he goes on to say, "It (the war) would not come to an end when they reached the great river that was supposed to mark their final destination."[12] For the layman soldier's perspective, we again turn to Koschorrek, a Wehrmacht soldier lucky enough to make it out of Stalingrad prior to its consumption by the Red Army. As his unit motored west, he wrote, "A really disheartening feeling comes over me. I would prefer to just get off the vehicle and disappear, as many have already done. It's not that I am a coward, but the retreat from the Russians, the soldiers around me with their frightened, pale faces, many of them without weapons, all add up to a very uneasy feeling."[13]

For those that did not have the fortune of making it home, the feeling of having their army as well as their held turf literally evaporate around them is nearly impossible to imagine. Koschorrek's mention of disappearing and unease would turn to brutal terror for many; of the 90,000 6th Army soldiers that eventually surrendered on the outskirts of Stalingrad, only 6,000 ever saw home again. In the Caucasus Mountains, few remnants of German presence there exist; just like the Greeks in Afghanistan, nothing remains save for buried skeletons and lost, rusted weapons.

None of these points are made to take one side over another; moreover, a perspective emerges: the victor's history often negates the real reasons a soldier finds himself at the edge of the earth. Some of these rationales are bad and others, however futile, can be good or—at a minimum—pure. The vanquishers of World War II have been in charge since 1945, undertaking their own versions of limitless conquest, often without arms. Russia and her former Western allies, mainly America, are two sides of the same bad-luck coin; some sense a potential waning of their power in the near future. Regardless, not all frontiers are physical; when will the current masters of this world find their edge, and what will remain there after the collapse?

Endnotes

1. Sidebotham, Steven. "Romans and Arabs in the Red Sea." *Topoi*, 1996, pp. 785-797.
2. Kirchubel, Robert. *Atlas of the Eastern Front: 1941-1945*. (Oxford, UK: Osprey Publishing) 2016. pp. 114.
3. Haupt, Werner. *Army Group South: The Wehrmacht in Russia 1941-1945*. (Atglen, PA: Schiffer Publishing) 1998. pp. 183.
4. Ibid., 183.
5. Beevor, Antony. *Stalingrad*. (London. UK: Penguin) 1999, p. 100.
6. Carell, Paul. *Stalingrad: The Defeat of the German 6th Army*. (Atglen, PA: Schiffer Publishing) 1993, p. 101.
7. Ibid.
8. Celine, Louis-Ferdinand. "Louis-Ferdinand Celine, The Art of Fiction No. 33." *The Paris Review,* Issue 31, Winter-Spring 1964, https://www.theparisreview.org/interviews/4502/the-art-of-fiction-no-33-louis-ferdinand-celine.
9. Hughes, Matthew & Mann, Chris. *Inside Hitler's Germany: Life Under the Third Reich*. (Lincoln, NE: University of Nebraska Press) 2000, p. 127.
10. Koschorrek, Günter. *Blood Red Snow: The Memoirs of a German Soldier on the Eastern Front*. (Barnsley, UK: Frontline Books) 2011. pp. 30.
11. Ed. Freidlin, Seymour & Richardson, William. *The Fatal Decisions: Six Decisive Battles of the Second World War from the Viewpoint of the Vanquished*. (Barnsley, UK: Pen and Sword Books) 2012.
12. Beevor, Antony. *Stalingrad*. (London. UK: Penguin) 1999, p. 101.
13. Koschorrek, Günter. *Blood Red Snow: The Memoirs of a German Soldier on the Eastern Front*. (Barnsley, UK: Frontline Books) 2011. pp. 59.

About the Author:

Anthony Bavaria is an American dissident writer. His work can be found in Counter-Currents' webzine and Man's World.

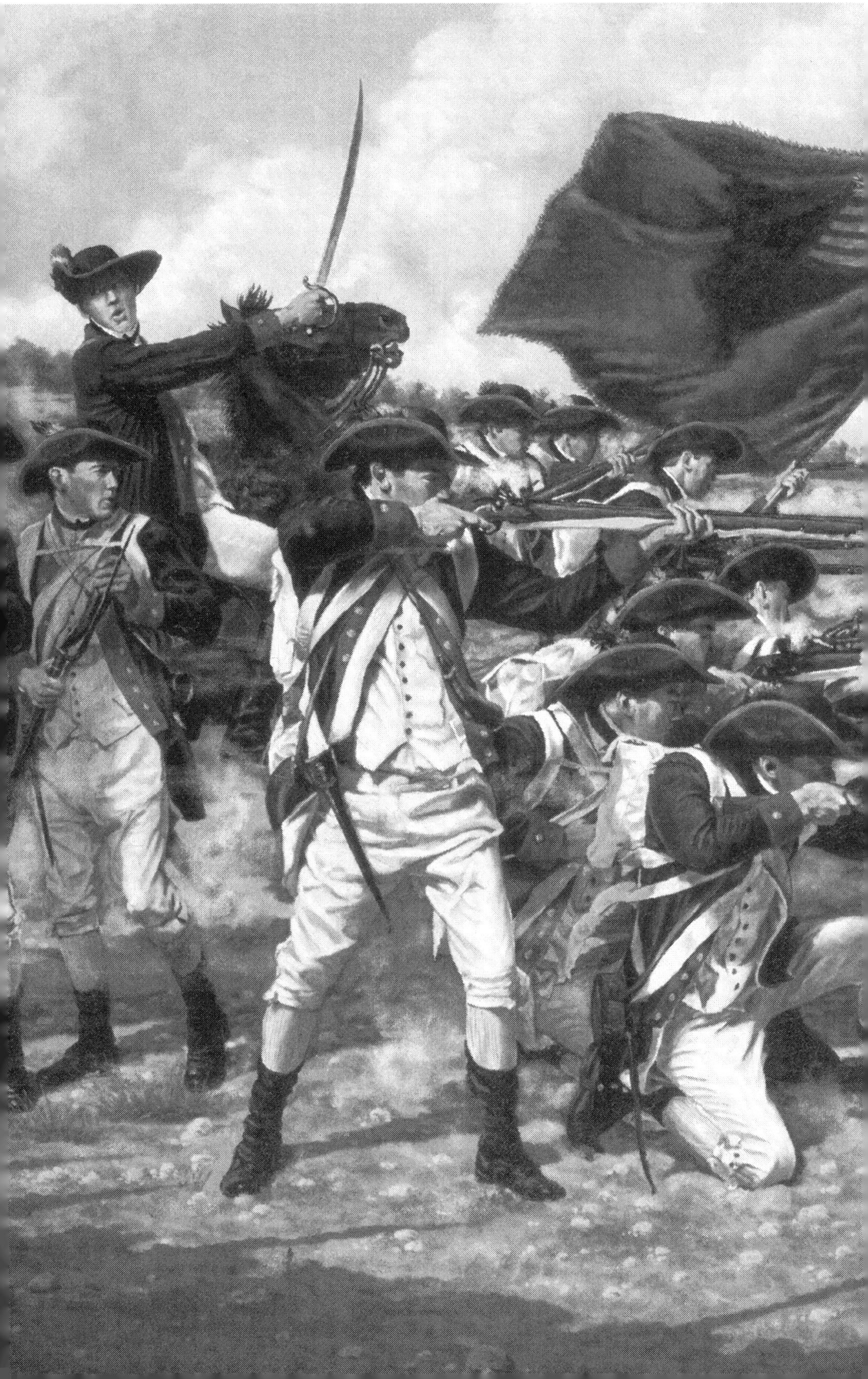

William Shakespeare: American Founder

By Banished Kent

"There is scarcely a pioneer's cabin where one does not encounter some odd volumes of Shakespeare."

– Alexis de Tocqueville, *Democracy in America*

In July 1787, a group of elite men met in Philadelphia, Pennsylvania to finish what they had started over a decade ago: founding the United States of America. Presiding over this convention was General George Washington, the warrior statesman who some had hoped to make king after gaining independence. Washington, however, was not interested in founding a new monarchy. Instead, after years of effete government under the Articles of Confederation, Washington and his fellow delegates had a much more difficult founding in mind: that of a republic. Inspired by examples from antiquity, men such as Thomas Jefferson, John Adams, James Madison, and Alexander Hamilton had by this point worked out the various critical components of republican government. Now they sought to materialize their vision.

On the afternoon of Saturday, July 14, after a session of the convention, Washington attended a stage production of William Shakespeare's *The Tempest*.[1] That the father of this new nation attended this particular play right in the middle of its founding is incredibly symbolic. *The Tempest* follows an exiled philosopher-king named Prospero, who uses magical powers which he calls his 'art' to tame the various factions on a wild island. By skillfully using his art, Prospero is able to reclaim his political authority and ensure a stable future dynasty by carefully providing for and educating his daughter, Miranda. Like Prospero, the American founders found themselves on an island of sorts, separated by sea from their mother country, and surrounded by both opportunity and danger. These men would likewise rely on an 'art' to cultivate an ambitious new regime: the art of understanding human nature. While these men certainly consulted various histories and treatises from the likes of Locke, Sidney, Thucydides, and Aristotle, the plays of William Shakespeare also provided crucial wisdom to the founding fathers. Particularly, both John Adams and Thomas Jefferson were thoroughly educated by the Bard's works. Combined, the two mentioned Shakespeare by name in their writings sixty-seven times. Their Stratfordian education is visible in their contributions to the American Founding.

Of all the founders, John Adams was perhaps the preeminent Shakespearean. At the young age of twenty-three, Adams had already come to see Shakespeare as the highest authority on human nature, writing in his journal: "Let me search for the

Clue, which Led great Shakespeare into the Labyrinth of mental Nature!...Let me examine how men think."[2] Even at this young age, Adams had been immersed in enough of Shakespeare's work to appreciate the value of his insights into human behavior. He owned a complete set of the plays, which he read repeatedly, going so far as to memorize his favorite passages. While struggling with a rhetoric assignment at Harvard University, having been mocked by his classmates for previously feeble speeches, Adams chose to recite a passage from *Coriolanus*: *"Look, sir, my wounds! / I got them in my country's service, when, / Some certain of your brethren roar'd and ran / From the noise of our own drums. / You common cry of curs! whose breath I hate / As reed o' the rotten fens . . . / For you, the city, thus I turn my back: / There is a world elsewhere."*[3] Evidently his performance as the spurned Roman warrior was stirring and changed his classmates' perception of him as an orator. This incident, however, was not the only time when *Coriolanus* was relevant during the American Founding.

It was common during the Revolutionary War for British regiments to stage Shakespeare's plays to benefit widows and orphans of soldiers. They usually chose to stage a historical tragedy with a definitively English setting, such as *Henry IV, Macbeth,* or *Richard III*. By contrast, American troops tended to be shown plays set in antiquity, such as *Coriolanus*. An American lawyer, Jonathan M. Sewall, wrote an epilogue to the play, which was performed for troops stationed in Portsmouth, New Hampshire. The epilogue is significant, as it tried to equate the American rebels to Coriolanus himself: *"But a majestic Roman, great and good, / Driv'n by his country's base ingratitude, / From parent, wife, and offspring, whelm'd in woe, / To ask protection from a haughty foe: / To arm for those he long in arms had brav'd, / And stab that nation he oft had sav'd."*[4] Sewell's epilogue makes clear that the Americans saw themselves reflected in this grand figure of Coriolanus, a Roman who had been rejected by his own city to the point of taking up arms against it. By making this comparison, the American fighters sought to paint themselves as noble heroes who had been mistreated by their own king. This provided war weary soldiers who may have questioned their actions with a historical parallel showing their efforts as heroic, even if tragic on some level.

Abigail Adams also quoted *Coriolanus* after the battle of Bunker Hill in a letter to her husband John. She wrote: "*Extremity is the trier of Spirits. Common chances common men will bear*"[5] hoping the words would provide an energizing spark of hope. During the siege of Boston she would also write to him, quoting Brutus from *Julius Caesar*: "*There is a tide in the affairs of Men / Which taken, at the flood leads on to fortune; / omitted, all the voyage of their life / is bound in shallows and in miseries. / On such a full sea are we now afloat; / And we must take the current when it serves, / or lose our ventures.*"[6] When the conflict of the Revolutionary War was most intense, it is notable that the Adams' turned to the words of Shakespeare for inspiration and encouragement. It is also noteworthy that their references during this period were heavily biased towards Shakespeare's Roman plays, set in a republic rather than a monarchy. They looked to Coriolanus and Brutus to see what republican heroes would look like.

It is evident that by 1776 John Adams was thinking deeply about what form of government the American colonies should adopt if their war with England proved successful. His and Abigail's tendency towards characters from Shakespeare's Roman plays shows a serious consideration of republican government. Indeed, in his 1776 pamphlet, *Thoughts on Government*, he writes "there is no good government but what is republican."[7] He goes on to describe a republic as "an empire of laws, and not of men." For Adams, good government must account for human nature. In his view, strong laws are needed to correct for the faults in human nature, both of the governing and the governed. Consider that Adams declared Shakespeare the "great master of nature" and the "great teacher of morality and politics."[8] Such a student of Shakespeare would come to see the limitations of relying wholly on the virtue of rulers. In *King Lear*, which Adams referenced on multiple occasions, the title character creates a succession plan where he gives the authority of kingship to his two wicked daughters, with the expectation that they will provide for him in his retirement. His only safeguard is that he retains one-hundred knights to himself. Lear, however, misjudged the character of his daughters, who immediately used their new authority to discard Lear's knights and throw their father out to die in a storm. From this story, Adams would have come to see the limitations of relying on the individual virtue of rulers, and the need for a more rigorous legal framework to uphold society.

Not only did Adams believe an "empire of laws" would restrain potential excesses of authority, he also hoped to utilize the law as a means of educating the people. In *Thoughts on Government*, he says his version of a republic would "[introduce] knowledge among the people, and [inspire] them with a conscious dignity, becoming freemen. A general emulation takes place, which causes good humour, sociability, good manners, and good morals to be general."[9] Adams, far from being an idealistic democrat, understood that common men had shortcomings just as frequently as noblemen. This would have been made clear to him in reading *Coriolanus*, as the plebians foolishly exiled their own defender. From Shakespeare's Rome Adams seemed to learn that a republican government is only as good as its common people. In both *Coriolanus* and *Julius Caesar*, the plebians are easily manipulated.[10] A republic which will provide for the "happiness of society" must then take serious efforts to guard against the tendency of the common people to be manipulated against their own interests. Adams' vision meant utilizing the law and the administration of government to promote virtue in the people and mitigate the weakness pointed out by Shakespeare.

Adams applied this understanding of human nature first to his treatise on republican government, *Thoughts on Government*. In this pamphlet, Adams outlines several principles which would later be adopted in the United States Constitution: separation of powers between three branches of government, a bicameral legislation, cooperation between Federal and State governments, and an independent judiciary. In 1780, before the Revolutionary War had even been won, Adams boldly drafted the Massachusetts State Constitution, which incorporated many of these principles and added a written Bill of Rights. With the Massachusetts Constitution, Adams nearly single-handedly pioneered a new age, paving the way for the republican governments of The West which would be formed over the next two centuries. The Massachusetts Constitution is the oldest functioning constitution in the world. When the Constitutional Convention was organized in 1787, they looked to Adams' work in Massachusetts as a model. Interestingly, Adams was not present for the convention, as he was serving as Ambassador to England at the time. Still, Adams had arguably created the pattern for the convention to follow, and further influenced the United States Constitution through letters during the convention.

Thomas Jefferson was also absent from the convention in 1787, serving as Ambassador to France. Like Adams, however, he also weighed in on the debate through letters, primarily sent to James Madison. Jefferson's influence seems to have primarily been to limit the powers of the Federal Government. For example, on June 20, 1787 Jefferson instructed Madison that the Federal Government should not be given the authority to veto laws passed by individual states.[11] After the constitution had been ratified, Jefferson persuaded Madison that the document was lacking in protections, leading to the addition of the Bill of Rights on December 15, 1791.[12] Where Adams saw a strong Federal Government as an opportunity to educate the people, Jefferson saw a potential tyrant that needed to be restrained. Here we can see a contrast between Jefferson and Adams, one that would eventually lead to estrangement between the two.

Jefferson seemed much more skeptical than Adams that a national government could be utilized to shape the soul of the people without becoming tyrannical. Indeed, in The Declaration of Independence, Jefferson claims that the purpose of government is to secure "life, liberty, and the pursuit of happiness" for its citizens, to organize "its powers in such form, as to them shall seem most likely to effect their safety and happiness." For Jefferson, governments exist to safeguard the individual, not to participate in forming him. These two founders developed two different political visions for the new nation, based on two different understandings of human nature. Yet, surprisingly, Jefferson was also a student of Shakespeare. The two friends both heavily studied his works for insights into moral and political virtue and came away with different lessons learned.

Jefferson began studying Shakespeare at an early age, writing quotations from the plays into a personal study notebook from the age of fifteen.[13] On August 3, 1771, Jefferson wrote to a personal friend, Robert Skipwith, with a list of books he recommended for a personal library. Jefferson felt the need to defend his inclusion of so many fictional titles in the list, writing that "the nature of the human mind evinces that the entertainments of fiction are useful as well as pleasant…everything is useful which contributes to fix us in the principles and practice of virtue."[14] For Jefferson, fiction was instrumental in learning to discern virtue from vice; to love good and hate evil. As examples, he pointed to two of Shakespeare's plays. First, he used Macbeth, writing: "I appeal to every reader of feeling and sentiment whether the fictitious [murder] of Duncan by Macbeth in Shakespeare does not excite in him as great horror of villainy as the real one of Henry IV by Ravaillac as related by Davila?" Later, he highlighted King Lear: "Thus a lively and lasting sense of filial duty is more effectually impressed on the mind of a son or daughter by reading King Lear, than by all the dry volumes of ethics and divinity that ever were written." For Jefferson, these plays offered profound teachings about human nature and natural law. In both cases, careful readers would gain an understanding of universal moral laws which could help orient them towards virtue. In another letter written around 1773 to Bernard Moore, Jefferson doubled down on his love for the Bard, saying "Shakespear[e] must be singled out by one who wishes to learn the full powers of the English language."[15]

These two American founders both believed Shakespeare offered unique moral and political lessons. They studied his plays, recited them in their professions, and drew on their teachings for their political philosophy. The two men were close friends for many years, even taking a pilgrimage together to Stratford-upon-Avon in 1786 to see the Bard's childhood home and grave.[16] Yet, by 1800 the relationship between the two men was severely strained. In a series of articles and discourses completed by Adams, the future Second President outlined then-controversial social views regarding hierarchy and status. In making his argument, Adams had quoted Shakespeare's Troilus and Cressida, particularly a line where Ulysses says "Take but Degree away; untune that string / And hark! What discord follows!"[17] Adams used Ulysses' words to argue that human nature remained constant, regardless of governmental form, and that failing to recognize and consider natural hierarchies would lead to societal decay. This argument would suggest that men are not inherently equal, even if granted political equality. This understanding of human nature led Adams to prefer a strong executive branch of government in order to avoid anarchy and promote virtue, as he previously outlined in *Thoughts on Government*. To Jefferson, however, this philosophy was too close to promoting monarchy. Adams' writings flew in the face of key assumptions Jefferson had contributed to the American Founding, namely that "all men are created equal".

How could two intelligent founders of a nation look to the same source for wisdom and come away with drastically different understandings? Here, perhaps, we can see the extent of Shakespeare's genius. As a case study, let us return to *The Tempest*, the play which Washington attended during the Constitutional Convention in 1787. It is fitting that this play was performed during the convention, because at the heart of this play are the very questions of human nature which influenced the formation of the American Constitution, and the divide between Jefferson and Adams.

At the very beginning of the play, Prospero uses his magic to sink a ship and bring its occupants safely to his island so he can exact revenge upon those who wronged him. The ship had carried Prospero's brother, Antonio, as well as Alonso the King of Naples. After washing up on the shore in the play's second act, one of King Alonso's oldest counselors, Gonzalo, is so impressed by the island's beauty that he imagines establishing a commonwealth.[18] Gonzalo's imaginary commonwealth includes "no magistrate", which implies there would be no laws. The people of this country would exist entirely in a state of pure nature, without commerce or labor. Gonzalo imagines that there on the island, nature would simply provide for his innocent population. He says, "I would with such perfection govern, sir, t'excel the Golden Age", referencing Ovid's Metamorphosis, which outlines a time where there were no laws or military needed as man existed in a perfect state of nature. Essentially, Gonzalo proposes creating a new Garden of Eden, and believes that by creating the right conditions he could dispense with the need for any political institutions. However, just a few lines later in the scene, after Gonzalo has fallen asleep, two other noblemen plot to murder him and claim the island for themselves. Gonzalo is only spared because of the magical interference of Prospero. Here Shakespeare cleverly shows the naivete of Gonzalo's vision simply by asserting that it is against human nature. Shakespeare then doubles down on the fallen nature of man in the next scene by showing the same flaws in a peasant-class man. Stephano, the alcoholic butler of the king, washes up onto the shore and nearly immediately determines to become the master of the island. He is worshipped as a god by Caliban, the island's indigenous inhabitant, who willingly submits to Stephano in exchange for wine. Caliban convinces Stephano to murder Prospero, who he frames as a tyrant. Within a single day on the island, Stephano, a commoner, accepts worship as a god and sets out to murder a magician, marry the magician's daughter, and establish a dynasty for himself on the island. Lest any reader be foolish enough to believe that commoners were more virtuous than royals, Shakespeare uses Stephano as a second argument against Gonzalo's Commonwealth. Such an idealistic state cannot function because it does not account for the ambitions of human nature. For Shakespeare, this nature is all pervasive.

The architects of the U.S. Constitution confronted this reality throughout their deliberations. While arguing for the adoption of the Constitution, James Madison asked: "What is the government itself but the greatest of all reflections on human nature?"[19] Here, Jefferson's protégé asserts that a regime is inherently a reflection of the founders' view of human nature. He continued, "If men were angels, no government would be necessary," directly confronting Gonzalo's vision of an anarchic commonwealth. "In framing a government which is to be administered by men over men, the greatest difficulty lies in this: you must *first* enable the government to control the governed; *then* oblige it to control itself"[20] (emphasis added). Madison reflects on the central questions of *The Tempest* by recognizing that a correct understanding of human nature will require a government which both restrains and is restrained.

Prospero represents this ideal government in the play through his actions. He uses his magical powers to restrain base characters such as Caliban, Stephano, and Antonio. These three characters seek to use violence to usurp power and establish their own political regimes. For his reign to endure, Prospero has to take decisive action against such murderous designs. Yet he also restrains himself. In the fifth act of the play, when he has complete control of the situation and *could* exact vengeance, he chooses not to, saying "Yet with my nobler reason 'gainst my fury / Do I take part. The rarer action is / In virtue than in vengeance. They being penitent, / The sole drift of my purpose doth extend / Not a frown further."[21] It is important to understand that Prospero is not simply looking the other way here, he does still retake his political authority and prepares the way for his daughter to rule, but he imposes limits on himself and spares his opponents. His regime is effective because he is capable of controlling himself as well as the other factions. Prospero demonstrates the proper balance that must be found for an executive to be effective at governing.

Questions regarding the powers of the Executive Branch were at the heart of the Constitutional Convention and have endured throughout the life of the United States. Federalists, such as John Adams, envisioned a strong Executive while Republicans, such as Thomas Jefferson, wanted a weaker executive and more decentralized authority. Even though both men admitted to learning great lessons of human nature and political philosophy from Shakespeare, they emphasized different lessons. Consider the differences between inauguration addresses given by Adams and Jefferson as President. In his speech, Adams reminds his audience how weak the government established by the Articles of Confederation was. He notes the weak government brought "melancholy consequences" including "jealousies", "rivalries", "contempt of public and private faith", "discontents, animosities, combinations, partial conventions, and insurrection, threatening some great national calamity."[22] He praises the still-new Constitution for its "effects upon the peace, order, prosperity, and happiness of the nation."[23] Jefferson in his first inauguration address, conversely, dismisses concerns about a weak central government, and instead emphasizes the limitations placed on the Executive by the Constitution, saying: "Sometimes it is said that man can not be trusted with the government of himself. Can he, then, be trusted with the government of others? Or have we found angels in the forms of kings to govern him?"[24] Here Jefferson has echoed the language of Madison's Federalist 51, and suggests man's fallen nature requires a restrained Executive. Jefferson asserts that a wise government would "restrain men from injuring one another" but then "leave them otherwise free to regulate their own pursuits of industry and improvement."[25] There is a clear difference in tone between these two Shakespeareans. Adams focuses on the need for order while Jefferson sees the potential for tyranny. They both believe in the principles of Federalist 51, in the principles exhibited by

Prospero, but lean more heavily to one pole or the other. Adams leans towards the need to restrain, Jefferson to be restrained.

Perhaps the great benefit Shakespeare lent to the American Founding was providing both visions. In Prospero, these two founders would have found evidence for each of their views. Jefferson could have seen a Prospero wise enough to restrain his own impulses while Adams could have seen a commanding Prospero who intricately directed the other characters. In reading *Macbeth*, Jefferson was horrified by the title character's murderous actions and subsequent tyranny, but perhaps Adams noted how weak and ineffective the pious King Duncan was. In *King Lear*, Jefferson could have seen the danger strong executives can pose to a peaceful society, while Adams could have seen the necessity of social hierarchies and the dangers of decentralized government. While Shakespeare certainly does not present a universalist moral vision, his plays are ambitious enough to capture the whole picture of human nature. The wisdom he offers to readers embraces the nuance of human behavior. He can teach Jeffersonian Republicans the dangers of unchecked ambition, yet turn around and teach Federalists to be warry of anarchy. He teaches, like Aeschylus' Athena, that proper government is "neither anarchy nor tyranny."[26] This search for a mean seems to transcend specific forms of government, as he offers settings in European monarchies, republics, and empires. Instead, Shakespeare suggested to the American Founders that human nature is a constant, never-changing frontier. Effective governance requires a broad understanding of this nature to properly hedge against its various manifestations. An effective regime cannot hope to change human nature and create a new Eden, but instead must anticipate human behavior and take precautions against the most destructive of them. The political division between Jefferson and Adams still exists in the United States to this day. The Constitution crafted in large part by these two men considers both their views and seeks to find a mean between them. Yet despite their differences and estrangement, Jefferson and Adams maintained some level of mutual respect. Their twilight years saw their friendship renew as they reminisced on their roles in the founding of America. Ultimately, the two were able to transcend their differences and recognize their pursuit of the same noble goal. Likewise, the nation which they helped to create would time and again find ways to reconcile its people, despite clear tensions in philosophy. This is not unlike many of Shakespeare's plays, which explore the bounds of philosophical differences within a common society. Here Shakespeare's philosophy evident in the American government, with noticeable tension between factions which are still bound together by higher goals. The Constitution, in the end, encourages both a strong government but also one that takes precautions against its rulers' worst impulses. The American people then are indebted to Shakespeare for the wisdom he granted to their founders. This debt can best be reconciled by keeping his words alive and thus preserving the understanding of human nature, the Founders' "art", which called the Republic into existence.

Endnotes

1. [Diary entry: 14 July 1787]," *Founders Online*, National Archives, https://founders.archives.gov/documents/Washington/01-05-02-0002-0007-0014. [Original source: *The Diaries of George Washington*, vol. 5, *1 July 1786–31 December 1789*, ed. Donald Jackson and Dorothy Twohig. Charlottesville: University Press of Virginia, 1979, p. 176.]
2. "[December 1758]," *Founders Online*, National Archives, https://founders.archives.gov/documents/Adams/01-01-02-0003-0003. [Original source: *The Adams Papers*, Diary and Autobiography of John Adams, vol. 1, *1755–1770*, ed. L. H. Butterfield. Cambridge, MA: Harvard University Press, 1961, pp. 59–66.]
3. Boller, Paul F., Jr. 2011. "The American Presidents and Shakespeare." https://www.whitehousehistory.org/the-american-presidents-and-shakespeare.; See also: *Coriolanus*, (Act III, Scene 3)
4. Shapiro, James. 2014. Shakespeare in America. The Library of America.
5. "Abigail Adams to John Adams, 25 June 1775," *Founders Online*, National Archives, https://founders.archives.gov/documents/Adams/04-01-02-0155. [Original source: *The Adams Papers*, Adams Family Correspondence, vol. 1, *December 1761–May 1776*, ed. Lyman H. Butterfield. Cambridge, MA: Harvard University Press, 1963, pp. 230–233.]
6. "Abigail Adams to John Adams, 2 March 1776," *Founders Online*, National Archives, https://founders.archives.gov/documents/Adams/04-01-02-0231. [Original source: *The Adams Papers*, Adams Family Correspondence, vol. 1, *December 1761–May 1776*, ed. Lyman H. Butterfield. Cambridge, MA: Harvard University Press, 1963, pp. 352–356.]
7. "III. Thoughts on Government, April 1776," *Founders Online*, National Archives, https://founders.archives.gov/documents/Adams/06-04-02-0026-0004. [Original source: *The Adams Papers*, Papers of John Adams, vol. 4, *February–August 1776*, ed. Robert J. Taylor. Cambridge, MA: Harvard University Press, 1979, pp. 86–93.]
8. Boller, Paul F., Jr. 2011. "The American Presidents and Shakespeare." https://www.whitehousehistory.org/the-american-presidents-and-shakespeare.
9. "III. Thoughts on Government, April 1776," *Founders Online*, National Archives, https://founders.archives.gov/documents/Adams/06-04-02-0026-0004. [Original source: *The Adams Papers*, Papers of John Adams, vol. 4, *February–August 1776*, ed. Robert J. Taylor. Cambridge, MA: Harvard University Press, 1979, pp. 86–93.]
10. Consider how volatile the crowd of Romans are in Act III, Scene 2 of *Julius Caesar*, being persuaded first by Brutus then by Antony.

11. "From Thomas Jefferson to James Madison, 20 June 1787," *Founders Online*, National Archives, https://founders.archives.gov/documents/Jefferson/01-11-02-0411. [Original source: *The Papers of Thomas Jefferson*, vol. 11, *1 January–6 August 1787*, ed. Julian P. Boyd. Princeton: Princeton University Press, 1955, pp. 480–484.]
12. "To James Madison from Thomas Jefferson, 20 December 1787," *Founders Online*, National Archives, https://founders.archives.gov/documents/Madison/01-10-02-0210. [Original source: *The Papers of James Madison*, vol. 10, *27 May 1787–3 March 1788*, ed. Robert A. Rutland, Charles F. Hobson, William M. E. Rachal, and Frederika J. Teute. Chicago: The University of Chicago Press, 1977, pp. 335–339.]
13. Boller, Paul F., Jr. 2011. "The American Presidents and Shakespeare." https://www.whitehousehistory.org/the-american-presidents-and-shakespeare.
14. "From Thomas Jefferson to Robert Skipwith, with a List of Books for a Private Library, 3 August 1771," *Founders Online*, National Archives, https://founders.archives.gov/documents/Jefferson/01-01-02-0056. [Original source: *The Papers of Thomas Jefferson*, vol. 1, *1760–1776*, ed. Julian P. Boyd. Princeton: Princeton University Press, 1950, pp. 76–81.]
15. "Thomas Jefferson to John Minor, 30 August 1814, including Thomas Jefferson to Bernard Moore, [ca. 1773?]," *Founders Online*, National Archives, https://founders.archives.gov/documents/Jefferson/03-07-02-0455. [Original source: *The Papers of Thomas Jefferson*, Retirement Series, vol. 7, *28 November 1813 to 30 September 1814*, ed. J. Jefferson Looney. Princeton: Princeton University Press, 2010, pp. 625–631.]
16. "Memorandum Books, 1786," *Founders Online*, National Archives, https://founders.archives.gov/documents/Jefferson/02-01-02-0020. [Original source: *The Papers of Thomas Jefferson*, Second Series, Jefferson's Memorandum Books, vol. 1, ed. James A Bear, Jr. and Lucia C. Stanton. Princeton: Princeton University Press, 1997, pp. 605–649.]; See also: "[Notes on a Tour of English Country Seats, &c., with Thomas Jefferson, 4–10? April 1786.]," *Founders Online*, National Archives, https://founders.archives.gov/documents/Adams/01-03-02-0005-0002-0001. [Original source: *The Adams Papers*, Diary and Autobiography of John Adams, vol. 3, Diary, *1782–1804*; Autobiography, Part One to October 1776, ed. L. H. Butterfield. Cambridge, MA: Harvard University Press, 1961, pp. 184–187.]
17. John Adams, "Discourses on Davila," The Works of John Adams (Boston: Charles C. Little and James Brown, 1851), 6:263–66; See also: *Troilus and Cressida*, Act I, Scene 3.
18. For Gonzalo's speech regarding the commonwealth, see *The Tempest* Act II, Scene 1, approximately lines 162-185.
19. Madison, James. 1788. *Federalist No. 51*.

20. Ibid.
21. Shakespeare, William. The Tempest, Act V Scene 1, Lines 34 - 38.
22. Adams, John. "Inaugural Address." The Avalon Project. March 4, 1797. https://avalon.law.yale.edu/18th_century/adams.asp.
23. Adams, John. "Inaugural Address." The Avalon Project. March 4, 1797. https://avalon.law.yale.edu/18th_century/adams.asp.
24. Jefferson, Thomas. "First Inaugural Address." The Avalon Project. March 4, 1801. https://avalon.law.yale.edu/19th_century/jefinau1.asp.
25. Jefferson, Thomas. "First Inaugural Address." The Avalon Project. March 4, 1801. https://avalon.law.yale.edu/19th_century/jefinau1.asp.
26. Aeschylus. *The Oresteia, The Eumenides*, See Lines 709 - 710. Translated by Robert Fagles. Penguin Classics.

About the Author:

Banished Kent is a Shakespearean disciple with interests in history, literature, and politics.

Also, John Adams' top guy.

Follow him on Twitter: @kentbanishearl

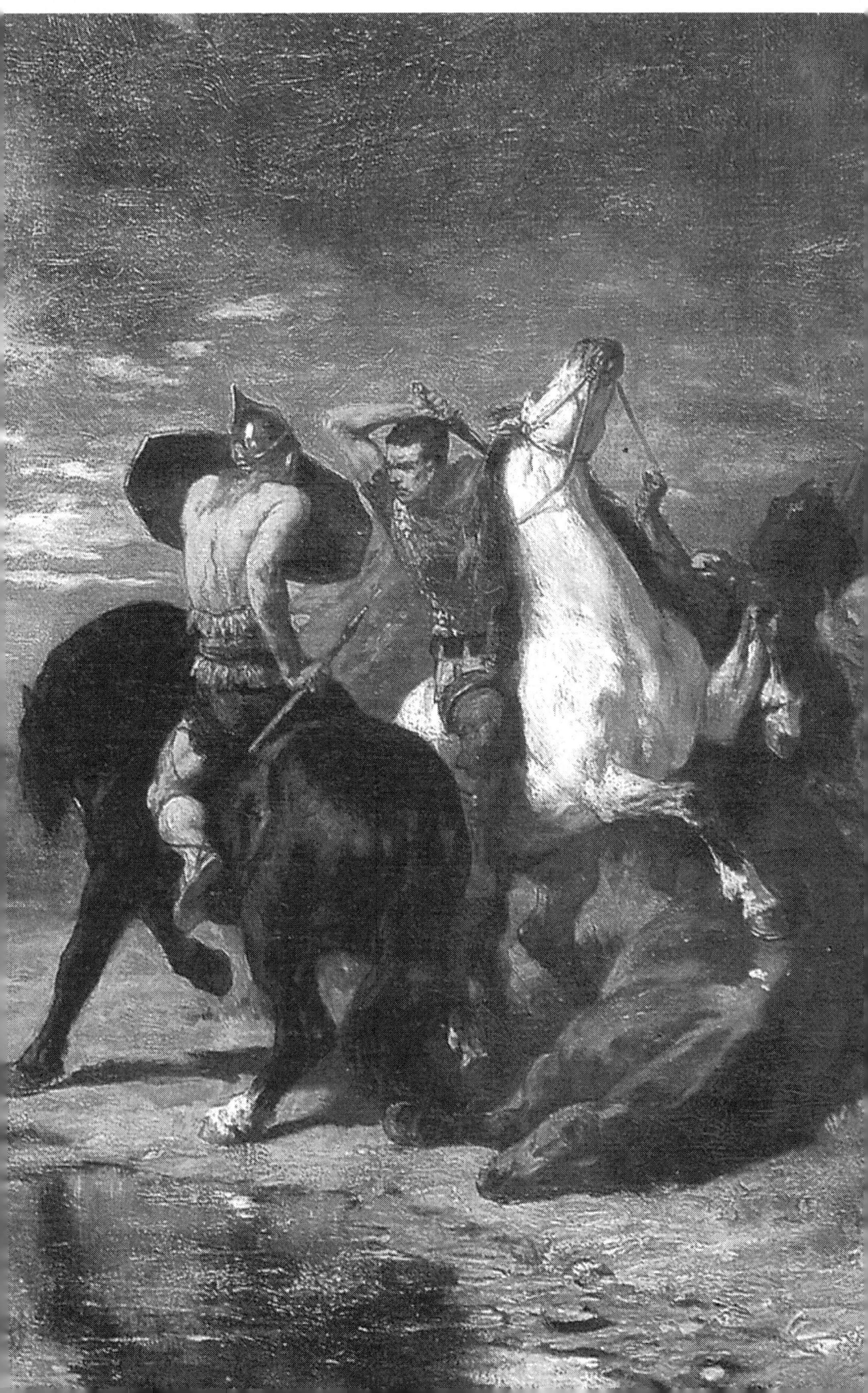

VENI, VIDI, VICI

Philosophies of Conquest in the Ancient World

By Mathew of Clermont

"Work was never pleasure for me, nor homekeeping thrift, which feeds good children. But to me oared ships were pleasure, and war, and well-glinted spears and arrows."

These words, placed in the mouth of Odysseus, sum up neatly the personal and heroic drive behind piracy and conquest. The Iliad, in many ways a portrait of the Bronze Age world, describes these notions quite differently than we do today. Homer approaches piracy as something that does not even require explanation or justification. To him, and to his audience, it was something that one just *does*; something all men feel a natural attraction to. Conquest, ventures into the frontier, subjugation of enemies, victory – to the Greeks, these were the domain of all well-raised individuals, the actions by which boys would become men and heroes would attain their inevitable peak.

However, it is not often today that one hears war described as "pleasure." As a society, we've been shell-shocked, broken from our supposedly centuries-long war-loving trance by the meat grinder conflicts of the twentieth century. Because of this paradigm, many today regard this aspect of the Iliad as barbaric, or at the very least primitive – they say that the valorization of war is something we've moved beyond, an evil left behind in the course of human progress. But this paradigm leaves out quite a bit of historical nuance, most particularly in the shifting concept of war and conquest between cultures and eras.

In the mastered and known world of the current age, our notion of war is primarily concerned with resources, "spheres of control." The frontier presented by war is therefore the frontier that opens up at the edge of commonly-accepted behavior; certain types partake in war partly because it is something unique, something disallowed in the normal course of life. In most cultures, violence is no longer an everyday occurrence, and permissible violence is even less common. So, the frontier presented by battle is the edge of civilized human behavior, of "normal" psychology and common day-to-day concerns. This type of frontier, sought by modern war-hounds and combat adventurists, is *not* the same that was sought by the Greeks, or the Romans, or even the British Empire at its peak. Therefore, our understanding of war and the opportunity presented by it cannot be applied to prior understandings and valorizations of combat. We cannot understand from our modern frame the way the Greeks thought about the call of the frontier, the opportunity presented by piracy.

The limited few modern adventurers and men-at-arms have difficulty expressing what it is they're striving for, because the very language surrounding the frontier and its call has changed. Namely, many of the words once used as positive descriptors have been reduced to slurs, polluted by neologisms and new connotations. *Pirate, mercenary, conqueror, colonist*: all of these words have become insults rather than the accolades they once were. So, in an effort to understand the rationales and cultural underpinnings of conquest throughout history, it is worth examining the frontier ethos of ancient cultures from within their own cultural frame. Instead of reducing all of them to simple plunder or a base desire for violence, we should strive to understand the call of the frontier as experienced by the Greek mercenaries who fought alongside Xenophon; of the Assyrian charioteers and spearmen who put so much of the Middle East to the sword; of the Roman legionnaires who marched through Gaul and Britain. Each of these conquering cultures has understood the call of the frontier differently, with concepts so far removed from modern thought that it is difficult for a modern reader to comprehend their thinking.

Before beginning, it is worth clarifying that in this case, "philosophies of the ancient world" refers to the views of cultures and civilizations prior to the Edict of Milan in 313 AD. Because this essay concerns pre-Christian moral systems, this framework, though atypical, is particularly useful. After the Christianization of Rome, old methods of philosophizing about conquest became intermingled with the Christian missionary spirit; here, the goal is to examine the belief systems of frontiersmen prior to Christian thought, which is more familiar to modern readers. Christian concepts of conquest and the frontier are fascinating and instructive, but would require a separate essay.

The Frontier as Chaos to be Ordered

The Assyrian Empire is perhaps misunderstood in modern discourse. Like the later Mongolian empire, the Assyrians have come to be known as a culture dedicated almost purely to conquest. Their advanced military structure and technology seems to contrast with almost cartoonishly barbaric acts of violence – covering obelisks in human skin, hanging lips from city walls, etc. The Assyrian legions were some of the first recorded participants in total war, especially in putting down revolts. In order to discourage future rebellions, Assyrian generals would wage these campaigns of terror and annihilation as a policy.

But this practice of ultraviolent warfare was only one element of their philosophy of conquest – a view which would see echoes in later empires, but never quite as strongly as in Assyrian thought. The Assyrian worldview was starkly organized between order and chaos: "correct" (Assyrian) methods of life and governance, surrounded by infinite territory to be tamed and put in order. In the neo-Assyrian worldview (during their post-Bronze Age Collapse expansion), Assyrian kings saw themselves as orderers of this chaos – as correctors and tamers of a disorganized world.

When Assyrian charioteers and spearmen vanquished neighboring kingdoms, later putting down revolts with almost incomprehensible levels of bloodshed, they saw themselves as a 19th-century civil engineer might when clear-cutting a stretch of forest to install railroad tracks. People outside of Assyrian rule were forces of nature: trees and rocks to be broken in the name of imposing order. To enter the frontier was to enter chaos, and imposing order in the name of the Assyrian throne was the highest good.

Their military organization reflected this – quite advanced for its time, it relied on group cohesion in infantry formations and blitz tactics by charioteer duos, both massively effective against the dispersed formations they often encountered. Thus, in the Battle of Ulai and the conquest of Elam, *order conquered chaos*, a physical expression of the Assyrian worldview.

These complex battlefield tactics were supported by political strategies of settlement and demographic replacement; like the later American empire, Assyrian rulers would send frontiersmen to settle new lands and displace the local power of natives, and later roll over these areas with their military to secure the conquest. Thus, once military control had been secured, an

Assyrian tax base and way of life would already be established, and dissenters from their imposition of "order" would be deported. The Assyrians were perhaps the first to engage in the practice of deportation; this was again an element of their stark division between order and chaos, their obsession with placing things in strict functioning hierarchies. Unlike the Romans, Assyrian kings did not tolerate differing religious practices or unique local systems of government. Fiefdoms conquered by the empire would submit to Assyrian methods of order and life or be extinguished.

In many ways, this philosophy of conquest is the most "ancient" of the bunch. It was based on civilization existing as a semi-new concept, and even though the Assyrian empire bordered incredibly complex and advanced civilizations – namely Egypt – the Assyrians saw themselves as imposers of this early system of social order. There was little talk of "justifying" conquests, of "morally proper" excursions into the frontier... it was simply seen as correct to place lands of chaos and disorder into proper ways of life.

While later empires would see themselves as tamers of nature and wild elements of mankind, none framed the world in such stark terms as the Assyrians.

The Frontier as an Entitlement

While the Roman concept of empire is often likened to the Assyrian ethos just described, it is worth noting the differences between the two, and the unique perspective put forth in Roman expansionist thought.

While Roman emperors and legionnaires saw themselves as in effect "taming" the barbarian tribes of Gaul, Britain, and more, they did not see themselves as the original imposers of civilization. Unlike the Assyrians, they saw "civilization" –

particularly religion – as something that had long existed in the regions surrounding their locus of control. The Gallic tribes were labelled "barbaric" for their lack of advancement and material culture, not for their supposed anti-civilizational chaos.

This concept drew most directly from the Roman tendency to universalize religions, particularly within mystery cults. These organizations united the disparate pantheons of Rome, Greece, Egypt, Syria, and more into one "central" pantheon with different expressions. Therefore, almost any religious system (besides the oddity presented by monotheistic Jews and, later, Christians) could be incorporated into Roman society. Unlike the Assyrian conquerors (or, rather, vanquishers), they recognized the existence of something resembling a meta-culture, at least in the realm of religious thought.

A similar social framework was extended to foreign kings and emperors, though by necessity it was not exactly as harmonious. Roman thinkers (particularly military men) saw foreign rulers as *illegitimate* – cheap imitations of true rule: i.e. Roman rule. Roman soldier-emperors viewed the societies which existed at the edges of their empire as their *right*, something to be claimed and brought into the fold of *real* government. The barbarian peoples could then be re-raised into Roman life, and indeed they were; many such individuals were made citizens after years of loyal military service.

The broad cultural diversity of the later Roman empire in some ways shifted this norm. Divorced from the original sense of conquering outlying lands to provide for the Roman core, the frontier spirit of Rome shifted from an element of that society to its primary unifying element. Instead of a people, Rome became a concept, a principle. Rome *conquers*, Rome *trades*, Rome *propagates itself* – of course, via the influx of new peoples due to conquest and trade.

Though the blame is usually placed on Christianity, this deracination is particularly compelling as the *true* impetus for the fall of Rome. The Empire lost itself in its drive for conquest, physically (i.e. racially) as well as philosophically – lacking a distinctive core in both aspects.

Perhaps this should serve as a cautionary tale, against embracing the frontier as a *protocol* rather than something more strongly grounded in divinity or racialism.

The Frontier as an Opportunity for Heroism

Now we return to the Greeks – to the oared ships and well-glinted spears beloved by Odysseus. In the Iliad, the Odyssey, the Anabasis, and other great works of Greek literature, the call of the frontier is framed in perhaps the most honest sense: as something that calls to all men, a land of potential for heroism and vitality.

Many disparage the Greek city-states as *pirates* today, but to them this would have been a compliment, or at least an unremarkable designation. Piracy, conquest, plundering… all of this was simply what one was supposed to do in the course of life. The morality of the involved parties was irrelevant – the only relevant factor was who could exhibit more bravery, more skill, more force. Warfare and plunder were simply facts of life, but it was the vitality exhibited by participants that made them worth it.

Today we speak of one's "right" to a piece of land or resource. The Greeks saw this right as defined by force: whoever could muster more force and demonstrate more skill in battle had the right to everything he touched. It was a culture obsessed with the heroic ideal, with the innate drive for glory. This drive is fundamental to human nature, particularly to male psychology. Men are born with the desire to test themselves, to seek conflict, to dominate opponents, to conquer. The Greeks were unique in that they were honest about it. While later empires would appeal to service and duty, the Greeks openly acknowledged that men signed up for war to seek glory and eternal remembrance.

This ideal is best seen in the story of Achilles. No notion of "duty" or "service" characterized his actions in the Iliad. When personally scorned by Agamemnon, he refused to fight, retreating to his tent in a state of white-hot fury. This is almost unimaginable today: a soldier flippantly refusing to fight unless his claim to glory and plunder was acknowledged. And yet this was the Greek ideal!

When Greek soldiers ventured out into the "frontier", the unknown distance, they did so with the same motivations as Achilles. Plunder, recognition, and above all, glory – that tangible, physical thing, which to them could be found in the space between linked shields and clashing spears.

~

Perhaps, in a world so roundly made anti-heroic – a world dominated by bureaucratic, effeminate systems of control rather than any particular valorization of the ancient ideal – the next frontier will invoke by necessity the Classical penchant for heroism and vitality. Or perhaps this invocation will be merely incidental, in the service of a different goal, akin to the Romans or Assyrians; or, even likelier, something yet to be seen.

Either way, people will never stop seeking the frontier as a concept. Today, everything that drives this impulse is disparaged or decontextualized for the sole purpose of slander. So, in order to facilitate this exploratory, ambitious spirit, we must first step out of scolding neologisms – and endeavor to simply *understand* it, in the same intuitive manner as the ancients.

About the Author:

Mathew of Clermont is a writer based in the Appalachian hinterlands – "America's Illyricum." His interests include oared ships, well-glinted spears, and arrows. You can find his work in various mail-order pamphlets, advertised only in that region and occasionally discussed on local radio.

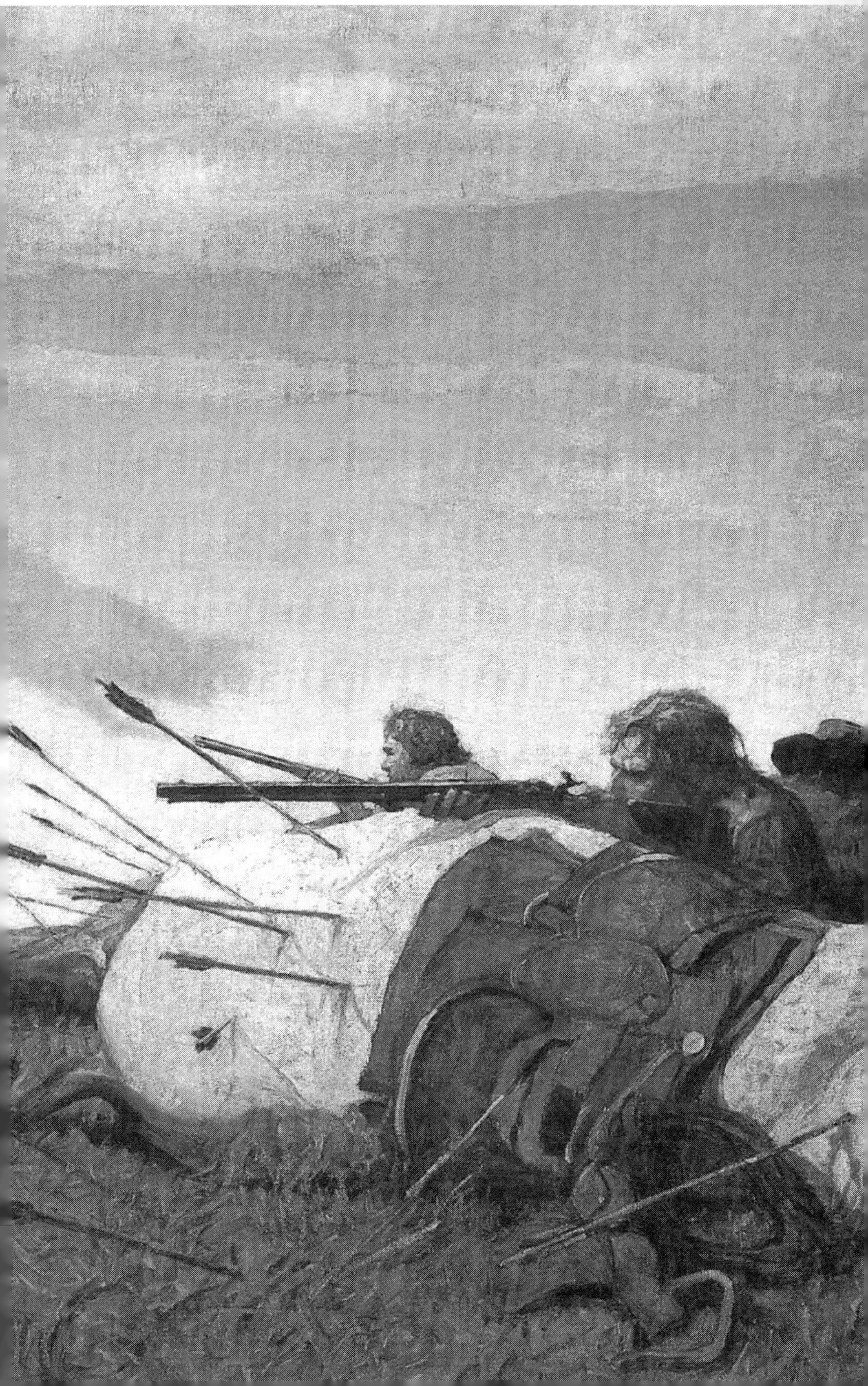

Ethnogenesis and the American Longrifle

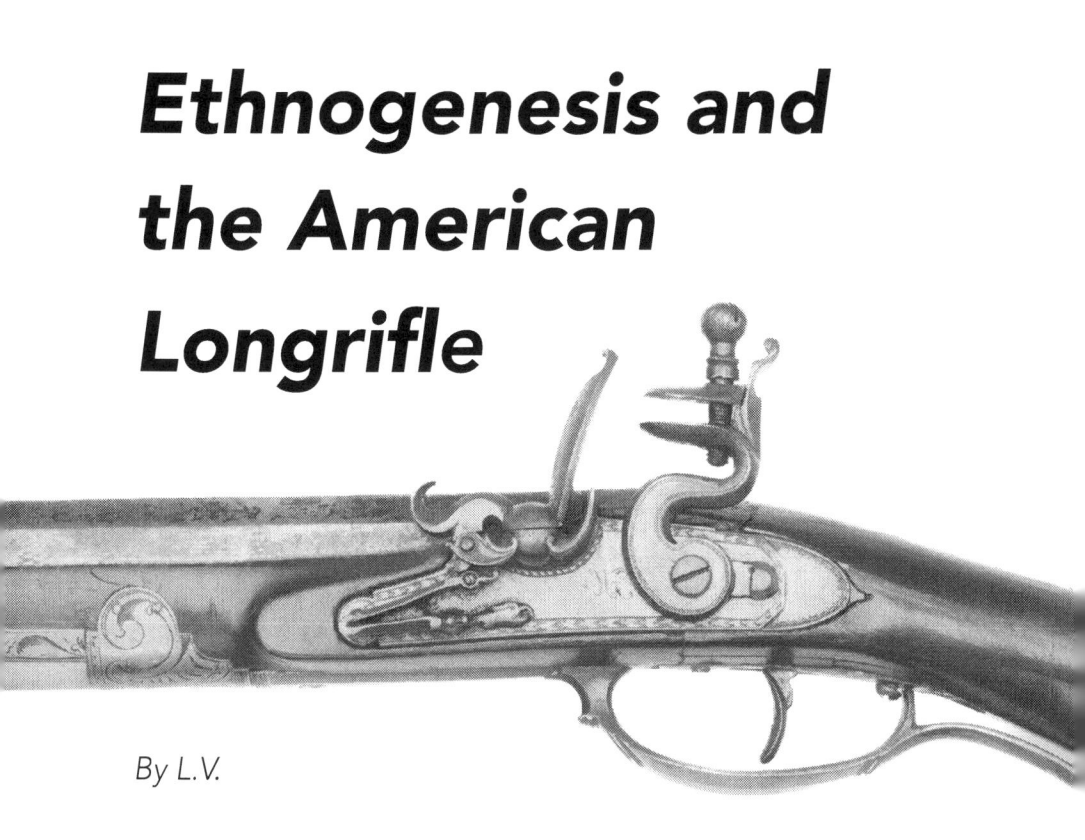

By L.V.

If there was ever a symbol to rival the eagle in America, it would surely be the gun. Fashioned by the early settlers for sustenance, survival and conquest, firearms have defined the American spirit prior to any constitutional declaration.

Perhaps no other weapon can lay claim to this esteemed role better than the eponymous American Longrifle. Predating the formation of the United States by several generations, this rifle forged its reputation as the tool of expert sharpshooters decades before the first shot was fired at Lexington and Concord.

It would fight alongside newly christened Americans on King's Mountain, fall discharged with Davy Crockett at the Alamo, shed brotherly blood in the Civil War and ultimately imbue a martial culture to a people who would one day claim dominion over the world.

In the early 1700s, the New World was a vast frontier of forests, savannah and competing occupational powers. Much of what is now the Continental United States was a series of revolving border disputes between England, France, Spain and deeply entrenched Indian tribes. Control over territory and the immense wealth of resources was settled in brutal skirmishes that ranged from lone individuals engaged in shootouts to the organization of armies thousands-strong.

Before the advent of a native gunsmithing industry most firearms in North America were imported under heavy scrutiny from British or French ships, intended for military outposts and the lucrative fur trade.[1] Smooth bore muskets could be purchased by early colonists for hunting and self-defense, but with an effective maximum range of less than 100 yards they never truly popularized amongst the citizenry.[2]

In the early 18th century, German homesteaders in the Appalachians developed a new style of gun boring that improved upon early Jaeger rifle designs. It was a natural fitting for the environment. *Jaeger*, the German word for hunter, specifically referred to huntsmen drafted into military service who were adept at reconnaissance, tracking and rapid ambushes that required a high degree of accuracy.[3] From felling roebucks to Redcoats, the Jaeger rifle evolved into a tactical lynchpin when it was first cast on American soil.

Originally known as the Pennsylvanian Rifle after one of its supposed birthplaces, it would take on many epitaphs including the Kentucky Rifle, Dickert Rifle, Widow-Maker, and American Longrifle. While the materials were similar to other firearms available at the time, what set this weapon apart was its novel rifling system. Instead of a smooth bore, gunsmiths would etch spirals down along the interior barrel of the rifle to cause the lead shot to spin upon firing. The spin would stabilize the projectile from veering in any particular direction, allowing for more accuracy at a greater distance: over 200 yards at two shots per minute.[4]

As the sarissa to the Macedonians or the longbow to the British, so too did the American Longrifle fundamentally change the way its practitioners operated on the battlefield.

Every aspect of the rifle was adapted to frontier life. Wood for the frame was hewn from indigenous curly maple; iron mined from local quarries was milled into longer barrels that increased muzzle velocity; even the caliber was shrunk to .32 caliber to maximize the limited lead ammunition that could be carried out to the backcountry.[5]

For gamesmen these technological advancements meant they could extend their hunting excursions and go after larger prey from safer vantage points. The impact this had on the colonies cannot be understated. Taming the land of natural predators and arming homesteads with accurate, easy-to-use rifles led to an influx of settlers moving into once-dangerous regions outside the realm of port cities. This eventually allowed them to develop a bustling network of communities with economic and political independence.

With every household now a potential sniper's nest, it became harder for the British occupational forces governing the 13 Colonies to enforce their rule. Gun control and seizures were met with violent resistance until the powder keg burst into the American Revolution, a movement only possible thanks to a dedicated minority of armed patriots.

It became integral to the survival of this new nation to ensure that its citizens were well-practiced in the maintenance and operation of their weapons. Regular training exercises augmented the difficult living environment, quickly earning Americans a reputation as sharpshooters.[6]

Ambushes and constant harassment from guerrilla forces severely impacted British supply lines, while Continental regulars could plot and simultaneously avoid traps due to their familiarity with the region's geography.

One of the most famous examples of these new tactics was the march and subsequent Battle of Kings Mountain.

In 1880, following a series of defeats at the hands of the British, including the devastating Siege of Charleston and the Waxhaws Massacre, American forces in Appalachia were scattered and on the run. The British appointed Major Patrick Ferguson to recruit Loyalist militias and crack down on dissent rising across the Carolinas. This was a task he reveled in, proclaiming he would "march over the mountains, hang their leaders, and lay their country to waste with fire and sword."[7]

This warning stirred the locals to action, who mustered their forces and began organizing scouting parties to track the movements of the growing Loyalist militia. "Overmountain Men," Appalachian frontiersmen so-called for their rugged endurance and mastery of the surrounding hill country, joined with the Patriot forces and began harrying the Loyalists camping in the area.

They soon learned that Ferguson was gathering his troops in South Carolina on Kings Mountain, a natural fortress that rose up out of the forests and would provide any heavily provisioned company difficulty to ascend. Luckily, these Overmountain Men and accompanying Patriots were equipped with American Longrifles and other light arms. The combined force of over 900 would make a heroic march of 330 miles in only 13 days in the lead up to the conflict on October 7th.

Not expecting a force of this magnitude to reach them so soon, Ferguson had neglected to set up fortifications and was caught unawares when American snipers began firing from their forested positions. Deployed into a Pincer Movement on both sides of the mountain, the Overmountain Men had been instructed by Col. Isaac Shelby, "Don't wait for the word of command. Let each one of you be your own officer and do the very best you can."[8]

The level of trust to carry out such a complicated maneuver when outnumbered by a foe on superior terrain is almost unimaginable. However, the level of autonomy that Patriot commanders expected of their troops proved to be deserved as every man fought independently to unhouse the Loyalist encampment.

Loyalist casualties reached 90% and Major Ferguson himself was killed in action with seven bullet holes placed deliberately upon his body by the Overmountain Men. Among them was John Crockett, father of the famed Davy Crockett, who would no doubt share with his son the experience of tracking and overwhelming the enemy using his intimate knowledge of the Appalachia countryside.

The Battle of Kings Mountain was an important turning point for the war, boosting American morale and striking fear into the hearts of the British forces remaining in the Carolinas. Future President Herbert Hoover would remark, "Here less than a thousand men, inspired by the urge of freedom, defeated a superior force entrenched in this strategic position…It was a little army and a little battle, but it was of mighty portent."[9]

Later campaigns would see the Americans transformed into well-equipped armies of capable marksmen with an ardent desire for independence. Decisive victories such as the Battle of New Orleans under the command of Andrew Jackson would inspire folk songs like "The Hunters of Kentucky," pointing to the already legendary skill of American riflemen.

It's important to note that unlike the British regulars, American forces were not generally career soldiers but ordinary volunteers whose supplies were reinforced through hunting and subsisting off of the land.[10] Integral to the success of their early guerrilla strategy was their ability to provide for themselves using only their own kit: A task made easier with a longrifle that could be forged, maintained and supplied from nearly every small town in the colonies.

One of the most famous proponents of the longrifle was the folk hero Davy Crockett. Known for his larger-than-life adventures in the American wilderness, Crockett first rose to renown under the command of Andrew Jackson in the Creek War of 1813 where he enlisted as a scout and spent much of his time hunting game for the army.[11]

Much has been told, retold and exaggerated about Crockett's life, nevertheless what is clear is that he was an expert sharpshooter and spent much of his life on lengthy expeditions carrying American Longrifles. Eventually rising to the U.S. House of Representatives, this "Coonskin Congressman" was gifted an ornate longrifle upon his departure from politics due to his professed love for the firearm that had already shaped much of America.[12] Little did he know that its greatest role had yet to arrive, nor that it would be memorialized in his own hands.

Political disagreements with President Jackson over government overreach led Crockett westward to the emerging Republic of Texas. His youngest daughter, Matilda, would later recall of him, "He was dressed in his hunting suit, wearing a coonskin cap, and carried a fine rifle presented to him by friends in Philadelphia. ... He seemed very confident the morning he went away that he would soon have us all to join him in Texas."[13]

For several decades preceding this, American settlers had been flowing into the badlands of northern Mexico, and would often find themselves targeted by authorities and bandits alike. By 1836 the Texas breakaway movement had begun in earnest, driving out many of the troops stationed in the area before Mexico decided to retaliate with unmitigated force.

Crockett arrived at the Alamo Mission near modern-day San Antonio in early February 1836, where a small garrison of roughly 200 men were stationed under the command of James Bowie and William B. Travis.[14] Supplies were already low when scouts reported an army 1,500 strong were arriving to place the mission under siege. It was expected the outpost would last no longer than four days.

On March 5th, a full twelve days after the siege began, it is said that Travis unsheathed his saber to draw a line in the sand. The garrison had kept the Mexican army at bay longer than anyone had expected thanks to their deadly sniping of encroaching forces. Now he offered every man a choice between survival and dying for the cause. There are no verified accounts of any man deserting his post: they would die with their rifles in hand.

The legendary battle came the following dawn in what has become part of the foundational ethos of Texas and the defiant American spirit. Songs, books, and movies have immortalized Davy Crockett's last stand: Of him firing until ammunition ran out, and going down swinging his American Longrifle until the very end. It is said his body was found surrounded by 16 dead Mexican soldiers.[15]

The garrison would be avenged soon after in the Battle of San Jacinto where Texians under the command of Sam Houston would decimate the Mexican army in fewer than 20 minutes with the infamous rallying cry, "Remember the Alamo!"

Annexation of Texas and the ensuing Mexican-American War would result in a total victory for the United States and deliver them more than half of the Mexican territory on the continent. This land would later form the states of Texas, New Mexico, Nevada, Arizona, California, Utah, as well as Colorado and Wyoming.[16]

The cultural memory of the Alamo and the riflemen who fought there helped to justify the expansionist agenda of the United States. Here we can see the first signs that America was not accepting of half measures, but a master of its lands from the capital to the frontier.

The arc of the American Longrifle was destined to be a short one, as the people who championed it would be unable to adapt to the changes that arrived a single generation later.

Less than 100 years after the Declaration of Independence, America would fracture in the wake of aggressive statesmanship between the Union in the North and the Confederacy in the South. The fallout of the Mexican-American War and the dramatic increase in available territory inflamed hostilities. Principally, proslavery and antislavery groups were bitterly divided over whether the practice would be permitted in the newly formed states.

Tensions exploded following the election of Abraham Lincoln in 1860, and in February 1861 the secession of the Confederate States of America and ensuing seizures of forts and armories escalated into an all-out war.[17]

Initially the states on each side of the conflict mobilized their existing militias. Like the *adsidui* of Rome, new recruits were asked to supply their own personal armaments.[18] Many of them brought the American Longrifles that they had grown proficient with throughout years of hunting and soldiering in the War of Independence.

The Union would swell its ranks with new immigrants and recently freed slaves and form a blockade of southern ports, crippling the Confederacy's cotton-based economy. With a bountiful war chest Lincoln ordered the production of new rifles to equip his Yankee army, including the Springfield Model 1861. At a cost of $15 per rifle, the Model 1861s were mass produced with over 1,000,000 making their way into the theater.[19]

Cheap to make, quick to reload and easily accurate at 500 yards, the Model 1861 surpassed the American Longrifle in almost every capacity. By the time the Confederates eventually rearmed themselves with modernized arms like the Enfield, their inability to fund their forces coupled with several disastrous defeats had already ensured their ultimate demise.[20] There was nowhere left in America to hide.

Use of the American Longrifle declined after the Civil War, though the American gun industry would continue to grow. The Thompson Machine gun, or "Tommy Gun," found notoriety in the hands of Great Depression-era gangsters like Al Capone who would use the rapid-fire weapon in ambushes and bank robberies. The loud, devastating blast of a Tommy Gun made such an impression on reporters and movie producers alike that to this day it's still known as "the gun that made the twenties roar."[21]

During the Cold War, the foundations of a shared American identity collapsed under rising social tensions between racial groups and the loss of trust in governmental institutions. In the background of this period of disillusionment was the Vietnam War, which would have a devastating impact on American youth and create a rift between them and their forefathers.

The ubiquitous weapon of this Asian theater was the M16, an improved version of the ArmaLite AR-15 rifle that appears in many artistic representations of the war from the late 20th century.[22] Cheaply produced, the metal was stamped out as opposed to hand-machined and partially made of plastic, with a weight of less than 10 pounds. With a rate of fire of over 600 rounds per minute, the M16 was a tool beyond the fantasy of frontiersmen that came before.

Soldiers who had become well acquainted with this rifle in Vietnam returned home to a changed political landscape where their constitutional rights were beginning to be stripped away. In 1986, Congress granted the Bureau of Alcohol, Tobacco and Firearms (ATF) expansive new powers to regulate the possession of machine guns and other firearms in the US.[23]

The battle for gun rights has only intensified in recent years, becoming representative of the increasingly strained relationship between citizens and their governments. The Second Amendment reads: "A well regulated Militia, being necessary to the security of a free State, the right of the people to keep and bear Arms, shall not be infringed."[24] There are many who dispute that this right has been upheld in good faith in the present day.

When the American Longrifle was first produced it was an unspoken law that every man was responsible for the safety of his person, family, and property. An occupational government bent on oppression strove to deprive them of this security and soon became embroiled in a hotly contested war that left countless dead.

The survivors of this conflict depended on the longrifle for sustenance, self-defense and armed liberation. Suited to guerrilla warfare, Americans settled themselves in the hills, woodlands and bayous and refused to be expunged without a fight. They rallied to leaders who asked only that they defend what they hold dear, and reared a culture that prided itself on autonomy.

In the end, the artisans that crafted dependable longrifles couldn't outpace the mass production of cheap arms that allowed newly arrived soldiers to stamp their citizenship with the blood of patriots. It took less than 250 years for the descendants of the first Americans to be convinced to disarm themselves of their rifles, as well as their martial spirit.

Where does this leave the American Longrifle, this symbol of the frontier? Was its soul extinguished at the Alamo? Does it lie buried in a shallow grave at Gettysburg? Or is there another icon rising that can guide the hands of a once-noble nation?

Let us learn from the lessons of the past: a weapon of the people must be equally suited to their current state of affairs while also capable of adapting them for the coming battles they are to face.

In America today, most gun violence occurs between gang members with innocent bystanders either mistakenly struck or targeted for their perceived weakness. Faced with economic uncertainty, this weapon should be affordable, require low maintenance, use accessible ammunition, and be easy to gain a basic proficiency for. With these factors in mind, one armament has already found its way into the hands of many gun-owning Americans: the AR-15.

AR-15-style rifles closely resemble the M16 and its ArmaLite predecessor with the notable hallmark of a modular design, allowing owners to easily customize and upgrade their rifles for whatever purpose they require. Interchangeable parts and a healthy aftermarket industry for the AR-15 has provided it with a versatility for hunting, sport shooting, self-defense and more.[25]

While ammunition for AR-15-style rifles is plentiful, prices surged after mass shootings began to feature prominently in the media. However, thanks to its modular construction and growing popularity, this rifle can chamber a variety of calibers which are widely available in every major city and small town.

Despite intense propaganda from overreaching political forces, the AR-15 has consistently been proclaimed the most popular rifle in America with more than 5% of the population reporting ownership.[26] While more expensive than other rifles, it remains dependable and offers a plethora of personalizable options. Its light weight and low recoil makes the AR-15 especially suited for new gun owners to grow familiar with shooting. In short, there's a strong case for claiming the AR-15 as the spiritual successor to the American Longrifle.

The question that remains to be answered is if there is still a people worthy of arming themselves with not just a gun, but a symbol of independence. Besieged on all sides by enemies foreign and domestic, a nation has never been in such need of a citizenry willing to defend itself and its foundational values.

If they can prove themselves as capable, disciplined and fervent as their ancestors wielding the American Longrifle, then I believe the martial spirit of these United States will reawaken once more.

Endnotes

1. "Long Rifles." *The Buckskinners*, March 2020. https://thebuckskinners.com/long-rifles/.
2. Ibid.
3. York, Neil L. "Pennsylvania Rifle: Revolutionary Weapon in a Conventional War?" *The Pennsylvania Magazine of History and Biography* 103, no. 3 (1979): 302–24. http://www.jstor.org/stable/20091374.
4. Ibid.
5. York, "Pennsylvania Rifle," 305.
6. Orrison, Rob. "Militia, Minutemen, and Continentals: The American Military Force in the American Revolution." *American Battlefield Trust*, December 15, 2021.
https://www.battlefields.org/learn/articles/militia-minutemen-and-continentals-american-military-force-american-revolution.
7. Horn, Joshua. "The Battle of King's Mountain." *Horn Herald*, May 20, 2010.
http://hornherald.blogspot.com/2010/05/battle-of-kings-mountain.html.
8. Ibid.
9. Hoover, Herbert. "Address on the 150th Anniversary of the Battle of Kings Mountain." *The American Presidency Project*, October 7, 1930.
https://www.presidency.ucsb.edu/documents/address-the-150th-anniversary-the-battle-kings-mountain.
10. Backus, Paige Gibbons. "Getting Food in the Continental Army." *American Battlefield Trust*, October 18, 2021. https://www.battlefields.org/learn/articles/getting-food-continental-army.
11. Wallis, Michael. *David Crockett: The Lion of the West*. New York: W.W. Norton, 2012.
12. Ibid.
13. Cobia, Manley F. *Journey into the Land of Trials: The Story of Davy Crockett's Expedition to the Alamo*. Hillsboro Press, 2003.
14. Todish, Timothy J, Terry Todish, and Ted Spring. *Alamo Sourcebook, 1836 : A Comprehensive Guide to the Alamo and the Texas Revolution*. Austin, Tex.: Eakin Press, 1998.
15. Stiff, Edward. 1840. *The Texan Emigrant: Being a Narration of the Adventures of the Author in Texas, and a Description of That Country, Together with the Principal Incidents of Fifteen Years Revolution in Mexico, Etc.* Kessinger Publishing, LLC, 2009.
16. Gray, Tom. "The Treaty of Guadalupe Hidalgo." *National Archives*, April 25, 2018.
https://www.archives.gov/education/lessons/guadalupe-hidalgo.
17. Foote, Shelby. *The Civil War: A Narrative*. Vintage, 1986.

18. "Kentucky Rifle, USA 18th and 19th Century" *Irongate Armory*, January 9, 2011. https://irongatearmory.com/product/kentucky-rifle-usa-18th-and-19th-century.
19. Brown, Jerold E. *Historical Dictionary of the U.S. Army*. Greenwood Publishing Group, 2001.
20. "Small Arms of the Civil War." *American Battlefield Trust*, October 17, 2018. https://www.battlefields.org/learn/articles/small-arms-civil-war.
21. Helmer, William J. *The Gun That Made the Twenties Roar*. MacMillan Publishing Company, 1969.
22. "M16 rifle." *Encyclopedia Britannica*, May 25, 2022.
23. "S.49 - 99th Congress (1985-1986): Firearms Owners' Protection Act." *Congress.gov*, May 19, 1986.
24. U.S. Constitution. Amend. II.
25. "How Interchangeable Are AR 15 Accessories?" *Bootleg Inc.*, May 10, 2017.
26. Guskin, Emily, Aadit Tambe, and Jon Gerberg. "Why Do Americans Own AR-15s?" *Washington Post*, March 27, 2023.

About the Author:

LV is one of those most dreadful of stenographers: an essayist. Writing at the crossroads of humanities, obscurities and politics, he inquires into the values and customs that have raised the greatest civilizations to their zenith.

Follow him on Twitter: @LarpingValues

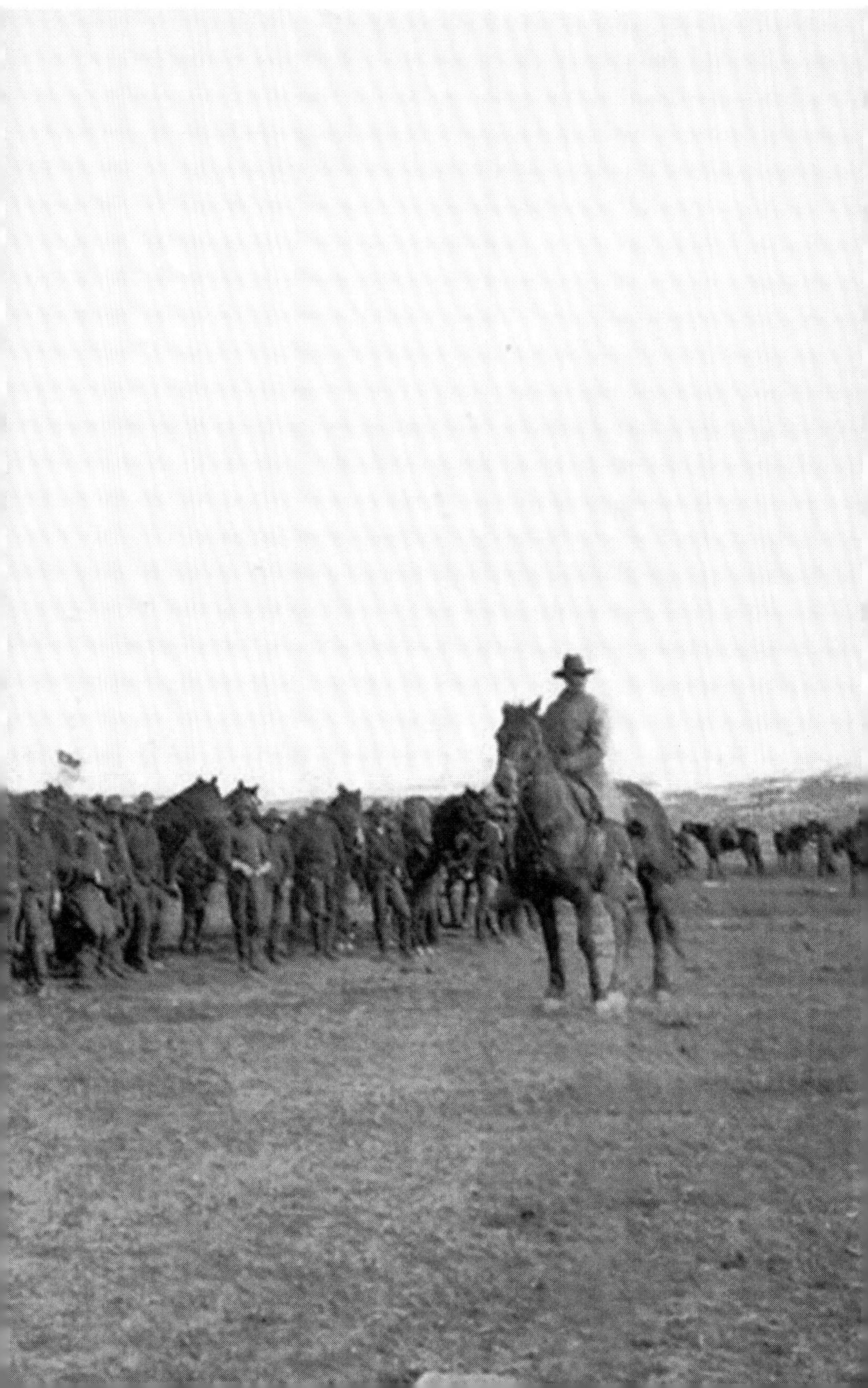

Justice and Force in the Frontier:

The Johnson County War

By Peter Iversen

The enthusiastically named Johnson County War is perhaps the best remembered of the range wars of the late 19th and early 20th centuries, despite hostilities taking place over the course of just over a week and resulting in only three deaths. It serves as an archetype of the genre: an escalation of violence in the background of a struggling cattle industry; mutual mistrust between wealthy cattlemen and small-time ranchers and homesteaders; and the conflict between squatters on the public domain and officially recognized homesteaders. On the frontier, the illegal actions of the cattlemen's posse were cured through political power and legal maneuvering, not dissimilar to modern obstruction of justice, and just two years later the incident lost its political salience. Its historical importance arises from its designation as the "class war on the range", though the Marxist overtones with this statement give an incomplete view of this conflict.

~

The opening of the Great Plains to American settlement proceeded gradually, through nearly forty years of treaties, warfare, and the constant incursion of White grangers and miners into Indian Territory. West of the Missouri River, America was closed to settlers, and Wyoming was divided by the 1851 Fort Laramie Treaty between the Blackfoot, Crow, Shoshone, Cheyenne and Arapaho, Sioux, and Gros Ventre, Mandan, and Arikara, but by 1876 Indian holdings in the state had been reduced to a Shoshone reservation along the Wind River in western Wyoming. Nearly 96% of the state was open to White settlers, but three factors prevented largescale migration: (1) the presence of hostile Lakota Sioux stragglers; (2) large bison herds; and (3) the lack of railroad access.[1] By the mid-1880s, the Sioux had been exiled east of the Black Hills, the bison hunted to near extinction, and a rail terminal built by Northern Pacific in Bismarck for freight shipping.

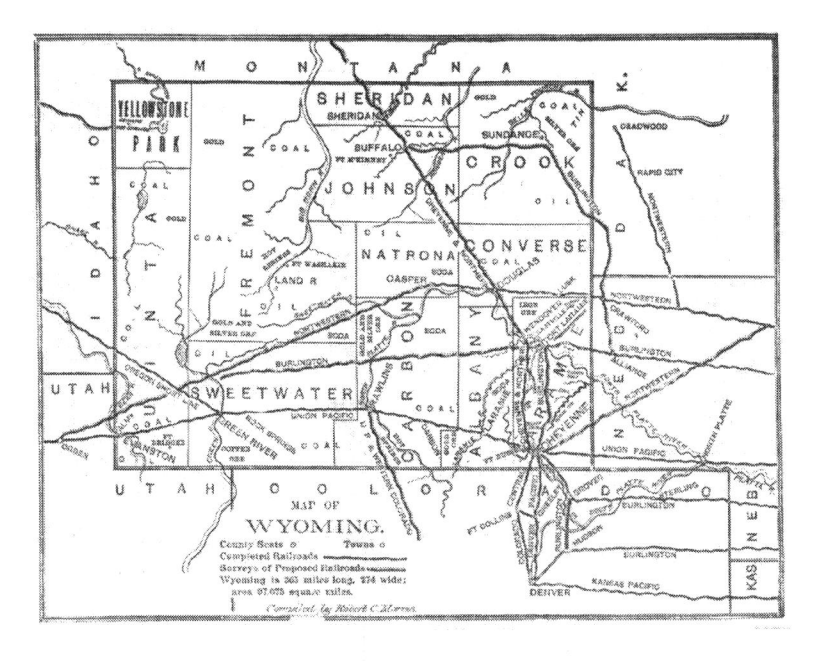

A map of Wyoming, with railroads marked that appeared in the Cheyenne Sun in 1890.[2]

129

The early history of Wyoming is defined by cattle ranching: in 1866, six hundred cattle were driven north from Texas, and on the eve of the 1886 winter, the so-called "Big Die-Up", over two million crowded the range.[1,3,4] Overcrowding was inevitable in the lawless frontier: the ranchers followed the doctrine of prior appropriation, whereby a cattleman would declare his intention to run a herd in a specific range, but for many years, herds were allowed to mingle and only separated in spring and fall roundups.[5,6] Worse, the cattle industry boomed, attracting absentee cattlemen from the Atlantic Seaboard and the United Kingdom who threw cattle on the range and expected them to fend for themselves. For many years, this system worked: the winters had been relatively mild, and the large herds were able to migrate hundreds of miles in search of forage and to avoid winter storms, but overcrowding meant that the rich grasses were mostly eaten during the summer and none were left to sustain herds through the winter, forcing them to migrate farther and farther.[7,8]

Technically speaking, the cattlemen did not have a recognized, exclusive right to the range, and once homesteaders began to migrate into the state, they claimed prime water access and put up fences to protect their claims.[5,7] The large cattlemen, to be sure, also took advantage of federal land laws: they instructed cowboys to buy homesteads, which they then purchased; they made claims in checkerboard patterns that allowed them to enclose more land than they were allowed; and they illegally fenced in both public land and the land of homesteaders. Blocked from their habitual migration, cattle died in huge numbers in the worst winter the state has ever known. It is unknown exactly how many were lost, with estimates ranging from 15 to 75% statewide, but the resulting low quality beeves, driven to Chicago in a desperate attempt to recoup costs, further depressed beef prices.[1,7,8] In 1886, the Wyoming Stock Growers Association (WSGA) had 416 members, representing $100 million worth of cattle; by 1889, membership had fallen to 183 and there was talk of closing the Association.[3,4]

Despite the beleaguered state of the cattle industry, the WSGA remained influential.[4,6,7,9] In 1882, at least a third of Territorial Legislators were Association members, and the legislative committee on the stock industry had been chaired by a WSGA member during the years of 1875—1890. The WSGA wielded this influence to pass the 1884 Act to Provide for the Gathering and Sale of Mavericks (Maverick Act), which had three effects: (1) to prohibit the branding of mavericks (feral, unbranded cattle); (2) to prohibit the branding of calves ahead of the spring roundup; and (3) to mandate a statewide general roundup organized by the WSGA.[3] This meant that cattlemen were forced to join the general round-up to protect their herds, as the Association claimed all mavericks and "dogies" (motherless calves) as their property to be sold at auction. Ranchers, if their cattle were marked as mavericks, were expected to buy them back and submit a sworn statement by a "disinterested party" that said maverick was definitely his to the WSGA to be reimbursed. Moreover, any cattle with fresh brandings found during a roundup were labelled as illegally branded mavericks and sold at auction.

The Wyoming State Legislature passed an act in 1891 to establish the Board of Livestock Commissioners purporting to vest the powers granted by the 1884 Maverick Act in the state, but the BLC's three members, J.W. Hammond, W.C. Irvine, and Charles Hecht, and its secretary, H.B. Ijams, were all WSGA members.[3,7] While some historians have viewed this as a surrender of power from the Association to the state government, a more accurate understanding is that it was an attempt—not fully supported by the members of the Association—to displace popular resentment of the Maverick Act away from the Association, while allowing the WSGA to continue to exert considerable control over the roundup schedule and rules. Even the funds from the sale of mavericks were not truly lost: under the 1884 law, these funds were used to pay for stock inspectors through the Association; under the 1891 law, these funds continued to be used to pay for stock inspectors, but now under state employ, allowing the

Association to defray these costs. In effect, the Association was still hiring inspectors and paying them, but through a different ledger.

Tensions between the cattlemen and the homesteaders, variously farmers and small-time ranchers, continued to grow. The losses incurred during the Big Die-Up forced the remaining cattlemen and ranch managers to be especially wary of rustlers, which were at one point an accepted part of the cattle business, but now represented a serious, and growing, threat. It is unclear how prevalent rustling was at the time: Mercer maintains that rustling was low; the cattlemen argued that the inability to prosecute rustlers proved that they were influential in the northern counties; Brown compromises, pointing to the redefinition of branding mavericks as "rustling" on the one hand, while also positing that cowboys laid-off after the Big Die-Up may have turned to rustling, and that the Bighorn Mountains were a rustler hideout for the mysterious "Red Sash Gang".[1,5,7,10]

However, it must be pointed out that the branding of mavericks was a widely accepted practice, and that managers paid cowboys between $2-5 per maverick branded.[1,7] Rather, it is more likely that the law was not recognized as valid in the northern counties and cowboys continued to practice their "right" to brand mavericks. Moreover, if rustling was rare, as Mercer insists, who was lying? The ranch managers and foremen may have misrepresented the number of cattle in the herd, discreetly keeping a handful for their own, and blaming the discrepancy on illusory rustlers. The ranch managers or owners may have explained away poor performance to their investors as depredations from cattle thieves.

Somewhat less clear is the impact of the sudden rash of labor strikes after the end of the Civil War. Of particular importance to the cattlemen's economic interest are those relating to the railroad, considering that freight shipping to the meat markets in Chicago was vital to their industry. Before 1892, there were four: the Great Railroad Strike of 1877, the Camp Dump Strike of 1883, the Great Southwest Railroad Strike of 1886, and the Burlington Railroad Strike of 1888. Additionally, the Haymarket Affair of 1886 was likely influential because it took place in Chicago. While labor strikes are unremarkable to modern readers, they were often illegal under the common law based on the theory that they were conspiracies (such as unions agreeing on a minimum wage) or represented tortious interference (such as attempting to prevent non-union employees from working).[11,12] It was not until the 1842 *Commonwealth v. Hunt* decision that labor unions were first recognized to be presumptively legal, and it took until 1914 with the passage of the Clayton Antitrust Act for labor union strikes, picketing, and collective bargaining rights to be officially sanctioned.

These five strikes represent over one hundred dead and hundreds wounded during the many days and weeks of fighting, and they are distinguished by the involvement of federal troops, state militia and National Guard, local police, and the Pinkerton National Detective Agency as strike-breakers. Even today, Pinkertons are reviled as little more than paid thugs for corporate interests. The connection between labor unions in the East and the Wyoming cattle range is made explicit by the move by cattle companies to reduce cowboys' wages in the spring of 1886 in response to falling beef prices, leading to what Smith refers to as the only cowboy strike in the history of the northern range.[10,13] Jack Flagg, who features in a later episode, was one of the leaders of the strike, and was blackballed and denied work with any of the major cattle outfits. Instead, he claimed a homestead on the Red Fork of the Powder River, in the foothills of the Bighorn Mountains, and started a little herd of his own. Valid or not, he later gained a reputation as a maverick brander.

The increasing threats to the profitability of the cattle industry coincided with an escalation of violence on the range, perhaps inspired by Granville Stuart, a member of the Stockgrowers Association of Montana, who raised a secret posse in 1884 that is claimed to have killed up to 63 rustlers.[1] Similar to other cattle-sheep and cattlemen-granger conflicts, Stuart was accused of serving the cattle barons to drive small ranchers and sheepherders from the range. In 1889, "Cattle Kate Maxwell" and Jim Averill were lynched along the Sweetwater River, ostensibly because Maxwell received stolen calves in exchange for sexual favors, a claim which later historians believe was slander intended to make her an unsympathetic victim.[1,7,14] Rather, it stemmed from a conflict between the pair and Albert John Bothwell, a wealthy cattlemen who repeatedly attempted to purchase their homestead claims, which commanded a priceless position along the Sweetwater River and blocked cattle access to water.

Tom Waggoner was a horse-raiser suspected of rustling because of the rapid growth of his herd. On the morning of June 4, 1891, he was kidnapped from his home under the presence of serving a warrant, and his body was later found in a gulch on June 12. Orley E. Jones and John A. Tisdale (apparently, no relation to John N. Tisdale) were murdered while traveling on November 28, and Frank Canton was accused and arrested of the crime, but later released. By the time additional evidence had arrived, he had left the state. When he returned to Wyoming in March 1892, he was served, given a hearing, and released on bond.

Nathan Champion, a well-known cowboy who rejected cattlemen's claim to exclusive access to the public range land, had roped and branded mavericks during the 1891 spring roundup, in open violation of the Maverick Act.[13] The same year, he had provoked a confrontation with the cattle baron John N. Tisdale by driving a herd into the same canyon. Tisdale, fearful that Champion would be able to surreptitiously steal cattle in the confusion, fled the canyon. On November 1, 1891, a group of four men entered Champion's cabin, intending to kill him, but a firefight broke out and they were driven away.[7] Frank Canton, Joe Elliott, and Tom Smith, WSGA stock detectives, and Fred Coates, Marshal of the city of Sundance, Wyoming, were accused, and although Elliott was arrested for attempted murder, he was later released. Champion had a reputation as a rustler, with claims that he was the leader of the "Red Sash Gang", but Davis argues that this, like the claims about Maxwell, were slander.[1,7,14] Even Willis van Devanter, a prominent lawyer, admitted in a letter to Senator Joseph M. Carey that there was no proof that he was a rustler, only his personal belief that he was one.[15]

Many events seemed to threaten the hegemonic position of the Wyoming Stock Growers Association and its members, but if there was a single precipitating event that spurred the "invasion", it is likely the formation of the Northern Wyoming Farmers and Stock Growers Association in late 1891, representing the "rustlers" of Johnson County. In 1892, it announced that it would hold a competing roundup starting on May 1, a month ahead of the WSGA general roundup on June 1, and led by Nate Champion, in direct opposition to state law.[5,7,13] The practical importance of this announcement is that it would provide an entire month for Johnson County roundup officials to brand mavericks and steal calves, denying substantial profits to the large cattlemen. Before the Big Die-Up, the cattlemen may have been content to combat this in the courts, but afterwards, still reeling from the near collapse of the Association and continuing poor steer prices in Chicago, they reacted forcefully.

However the decision was made, the members of the exclusive Cheyenne Club, traditionally limited to two hundred members of the WSGA, made the decision to bring together a posse to eliminate the "rustlers" in the north country. A budget of $100,000 ($3.3 million in 2023 dollars) was collected and a search commission sent out in all directions to bring back hired guns. They succeeded in bringing together twenty-two hired guns from Texas, one from Idaho, six stock detectives from the WSGA, and twenty cattlemen. Most notable of the party was W.J. Clarke, the State Water Commissioner, William C. Irvine, the manager of the Ogllala Land and Cattle Company and a state politician, William E. Guthrie, a cattleman and state legislator, and Frank Wolcott, manager of the Tolland Cattle Company and Justice of the Peace of Carbon County. Two of the cattle detectives, Frank Canton and Joe Elliot, had been accused of the killings of John A. Tisdale and Orley E. Jones, as well as the attempted murder of Nate Champion, in 1891. The party was equipped with a surgeon, Dr. Penrose, and accompanied by two reporters, Sam T. Clover from the Chicago Herald and Ed Towse of the Cheyenne Sun.

The party, described by sympathetic accounts as "regulators" and by antagonistic accounts as "invaders", enjoyed an environment conducive to extra-judicial killings of accused rustlers. As Mercer relates, convincing Governor Barber to support the "regulators" was vital, and a number of influential cattlemen met with him constantly to ensure it.[7] Two of them, William C. Irvine and Frank Wolcott, would later participate in the range war. George W. Baxter, president and manager of the Western Union Beef Company, had employed another invader, Mike Shonsey, as foreman. J. W. Hammond and Hiram B. Ijams were both on the Board of Livestock Commissioners, and Ijams was also Secretary of the WSGA. Henry G. Hay was the co-founder of the Laramie River Cattle Company and Treasurer of the WSGA.

They were apparently successful, as Attorney General Frank Stitzer sent General Order 4 on March 23, 1892 to the Wyoming National Guard, instructing them to ignore requests for aid unless it came from the Governor's office, in direct violation of Wyoming law at the time which allowed county sheriffs, mayors, and judges to request aid from the National Guard in certain circumstances. Finally, publications in many major newspapers, including in Mercer's own Northwestern Livestock Journal, had decried the epidemic of rustling in the state and advocated violent solutions. The field was cleared, and the operation commenced.

The group collected in Cheyenne, supplied from Fort D. A. Russell in what Mercer describes as proof of support from the federal government, then took the train north to Casper on April 5, leaving by horseback the next day to the Tisdale Ranch.

Ed David, range manager for Senator Joseph M. Carey's CY Ranch, is accused of going ahead to cut the telegraph wires to prevent the "rustlers" from being warned. On April 7, Shonsey alerted the group to the presence of rustlers in the neighboring ranch along the Middle Fork of the Powder River, and the next night, on April 8, the entire crew descended on the KC Ranch. Two trappers, Bill Jones and William Walker, were captured as they left the cabin to gather water for breakfast, and Nick Ray, sensing that something had gone wrong, stepped out of the cabin where he was immediately shot. Nathan Champion, who had rented the ranch, dragged Ray's half-dead body back into the cabin and set in for a grueling siege. In the mid-afternoon, Jack Flagg and his stepson had ridden near the cabin when they, too, were fired upon and forced to flee up the trail to Buffalo. Realizing that a posse would soon be gathered in Johnson County, the invaders loaded a wagon with hay and set fire to the cabin. When Champion emerged, he attempted a brief dash to safety before being shot 28 times. To his vest, a sign reading "Cattle thieves, beware!" was pinned as a warning.

Returning to the Tisdale Ranch, a handful of desertions shook the crew, and the decision was made to move to the TA Ranch on the Crazy Woman Creek where they would mount a defense against the inevitable retaliation. Meanwhile, Flagg and his stepson, as well as Terrence Smith, a settler who heard the shooting, had ridden to Buffalo to gather a posse. Over three hundred men surrounded the TA Ranch, vastly outnumbering the cattlemen who had lost a man along the way: a Texan, James Dudley, who had been bucked from his horse and broke his leg, then sent to the military hospital to recover. Fortunately for them, however, their position was well-defended, and the Wyoming National Guard and neighboring Fort McKinney refused to aid the posse. The siege began on April 11, and by April 13 a device called the "go-devil" was built to breach the defensive walls. Built around two wagons captured from the invader's supply train, the go-devil was a mobile breastwork, allowing a number of men to approach the Ranch protected from bullets, where they planned to toss dynamite to destroy the wall.

Fortunately again for the cattlemen, the telegraph lines were repaired on April 12 and Governor Barber was alerted to the siege. Immediately, he sent a series of midnight telegrams to President Harrison and the two Wyoming Senators, Francis E. Warren and Joseph M. Carey, to warn of a state of "insurrection in Johnson County" and request a detachment from the US Army. On the morning of April 13, Colonel J. J. Van Horn of the US 6th Cavalry rode out from Fort McKinney to stop the fighting and take the invaders into custody. A brief negotiation took place, and 45 men were arrested. George Dunning had hid before being captured by Sheriff Angus of Johnson County and jailed; R. M. Allen, manager of the Nebraska-based Standard Cattle Company had already left the party after the events of KC Ranch and was later arrested in Buffalo; a Texan, Alex Lowther, had been shot in the groin and would be sent for later. Immediately, Sheriff Angus went to acquire arrest warrants for murder and arson against the cattlemen, but van Horn refused to surrender the prisoners to Johnson County, and Governor Barber refused to compel van Horn to comply with the warrants, instead instructing the Sheriff to send Allen to Fort McKinney.

Once in custody, the War had clearly failed in a military sense, and now the goal was to prevent the situation from spiraling into political defeat for the Republican Party, which had gained the identity of the party of the cattle barons. Willis van Devanter, a former justice of the Supreme Court of Wyoming, was tasked with organizing the legal defense of the "regulators" while also taking the responsibility of chairman of the Republican campaign.[15] As unsuccessful as his political efforts were in the 1892 elections, his lawfare made up for it. On April 18, the group was transferred to Fort D. A. Russell in Cheyenne, where they were allowed to roam the city, some even leaving the state entirely.[7] At the same time, the Deputy Sheriff of Converse County, Emerson H. Kimball, claimed that the two witnesses to the killing of Ray and Champion, the trappers Jones and Walker, had been chased out of Wyoming by lackeys of the cattlemen.

A famous image of the "Johnson County Invaders" taken in Fort D. A. Russell on May 4, 1892.[16]

Finally, a formal change of venue to Cheyenne was acquired in July 1892, and during the August hearing, a petition for relief was submitted to the court, claiming that Johnson County had not reimbursed expenses for the quartering of the prisoners, and that they could not be expected to repay them, despite contemporary reports that they were often permitted to leave custody on their own recognizance. The judicial term of court was ending, and the judge concurred with the sheriff, and ordered the defendants to be released on their individual recognizance. When court re-opened in January 1893, the Texans obviously failed to return, and with their best witnesses unavailable and the juror pool exhausted by van Devanter's legal maneuvers, the prosecution for Johnson County was forced to file a declaration of *nolle prosequi* and dropped the case against all defendants.

At the same time as van Devanter was fighting a legal battle to protect the cattlemen, there was a concerted effort to have martial law declared in Johnson County, the idea being that it would act as proof that the County was controlled by the criminal element and diminish the negative political impact of the Johnson County War. As early as April 8, there were rumors that the "regulators" were a gang of Pinkertons moving north to kill settlers, suggesting that people had noticed their provisioning in Cheyenne and assumed the worst.[17] Soon after the group was captured by the US 6th Cavalry, Senators Warren and Carey were attempting to convince President Harrison to declare martial law, which he firmly refused. There had been two major disturbances in northern Wyoming during the month of May: the murder of Deputy US Marshal and Johnson County roundup foreman George Wellman, and a series of fires at Fort McKinney that were blamed on arson.[17,18] The death of Wellman was, at the time, particularly contentious: Mercer claims that his death was orchestrated by the cattlemen themselves to act as a false flag, while the cattlemen naturally claimed that he had been killed by the rustlers of Johnson County while attempting to stop the illegal roundup.[7] However, Wellman was well-liked in Buffalo, and it was proved many years later that he had been killed by a local thug named Ed Starr, though the motive remains unclear.[14]

Two messages were sent, one a telegram by a group of six cattlemen, including Wolcott and van Devanter, to Senator Carey on June 1, demanding a detachment of "colored troops" who would have no sympathy for the White rustlers, and the second the same day from Senator Warren to Senator Carey requesting that he inform the Department of War of thefts and arson at Fort McKinney, as well as mail tampering.[18] At the same time, a group of twenty signatories, mostly cattle interests, including six invaders, sent a petition for martial law to Governor Barber, citing rustling, violence against innocents, the illegal roundup by the NWSFGA and resistance to an injunction against said roundup, robbery, tampering with the mail, and complicity with all of the above by the Johnson County authorities.[7]

While they failed in their attempt to force a declaration of martial law, two detachments were sent to Wyoming: the US 9th Cavalry made a camp along the Powder River, near a railroad town named Suggs; the US 6th Cavalry stationed near Fort Fetterman just northwest of Douglas. The presence of the Black 9th Cavalry, the "Buffalo Soldiers" that inspired the Buffalo Soldiers of the Second World War, naturally sparked conflict. The soldiers were "a bit turbulent in camp" according to David, which is tempered by Schubert's claim that this trait was common among all regiments of the US Cavalry of that time.[18,19] The involvement of federal troops in breaking the Great Railroad Strike of 1877 likely inspired some resentment among the citizenry, and there were some who were openly abusive to the soldiers, both the White officers and Black enlisted men. The greatest provocation was the presence of Philip Du Fran, a stock detective and one of the invaders who was supposed to be imprisoned in Cheyenne awaiting trial, in the camp of the US 9th Cavalry, having been hired as a guide. His presence led locals to assume that the soldiers were there to assist the cattlemen in driving out the homesteaders.

On the evening of June 16th, a Buffalo Soldier, Pvt. Champ, had gone into town to find a prostitute he had frequented near Fort Robinson, in Nebraska.[18,19] The woman in particular had apparently begun cohabitating with a White man, and refused him. Instead, Pvt. Champ went to a saloon where he met Pvt. Smith, and moments later the two were met by the White lover, who drew a revolver on Champ. The situation escalated, and the two soldiers were forced to flee the town, exchanging fire on the way out. The officers attempted to prevent the soldiers from leaving the camp again, but on the night of the 17th, a group of twenty snuck out to shoot up the town. The ensuing firefight ended with the Buffalo Soldiers being driven from the town with the death of one soldier, Pvt. Willis Johnston. The incident was a massive embarrassment for the US Army, and they ordered the two detachments to remain in their camps at all times before deploying the Buffalo Soldiers to Coeur d'Alene, Idaho to crush a miner's strike, a fact not lost on the Wyoming newspapers.

There is one final anecdote that serves to cap off the entire affair, relayed by Mercer.[7] The Western Union Beef Company operated a herd in Johnson County with Mike Shonsey as foreman. Finding the grass to be depleted in the area, George W. Baxter decided to drive the herd to Montana to find better pastorage. In the autumn of 1892, after the herd had been gathered, the count was a full two thousand higher than was recorded in company books. There were some accusations that this reflected a scheme to siphon off cattle for themselves, but Mercer contents himself with smugly pointing out that if rustling was rampant in the county, they should have noticed their herds diminishing day-by-day, not swelled by an additional two thousand heads. This anecdote, Mercer believes, proves that rustling in Johnson County, insofar as it existed, must have been relatively minor.

~

The Johnson County War, because of the clear identification of wealthy cattle barons and the Johnson County settlers as antagonistic parties in the conflict, has been characterized as a "class war" in Marxist fashion. Some concept of class warfare existed as early as the Corcyraean Civil War in 427 BC mentioned in Thucydides' *History of the Peloponnesian War*, Book III, Chapter 69—85, but it was not until the *Manifesto of the Communist Party* in 1848, that class struggle as historiography became widespread. This was expanded by Sorel's *Reflections on Violence* to distinguish between the ability of the state to use force as a presumptively legitimate power to create order and subordinate the worker beneath capital, which was countered by proletarian violence, properly understood as an act of revolt against the tyrannical system of wage slavery.

Under this understanding of the nature of the Johnson County War, because the state in the frontier is weak, capital interests take their place and can ensure that the law benefits them. In other words, the state prerogative is forced to conform to moneyed interests, not dissimilar to the way that the military-industrial complex is accused to steering American foreign policy today. This alignment allows the wealthy to leverage the full force of the state to legitimize their exploitation of the commons while at the same time strictly restricting the ability of small-time agents to profit at their expense. In this conjoined capital-state, these exploitations receive the benefits of sovereign immunity, and the exploiters are protected against lèse-majesté. In the 21st century, the ability of corporations to benefit from eminent domain, such as the infamous Fort Trumbull redevelopment project in New London, Connecticut that fizzled out in the 2008 Great Recession, represents the former. The latter was most vividly witnessed in the stock market manipulation performed to protect institutional short sellers, such as in the 2022 LME nickel market and 2021 GameStop stock short squeezes. This is echoed by Chomsky in his rejection of the slogan of free market doctrine as representing in actuality the imposition of austerity on the poor and protectionism and subsidies for the rich.[20] The Johnson County War, therefore, represented the exploitation and marginalization of the granger class escalating into the outright use of force by the "WSGA-occupied government" to force capitulation.

Juxtaposed against the Marxist interpretation of class conflict, however, is that of Evola and its later fascist elaboration. In *Metaphysics of War*, Evola outlines the traditional caste system of society consisting of, not unlike the Hindu caste system, slaves, a bourgeois middle class, a warrior aristocracy, and a spiritual elite. Warfare properly understood, for Evola, is the combat of the soul to transcend the mere biology of human existence, but as society is reordered away from this ideal hierarchy, the nature of war changes and the society begins to fall into decline.[21] Similarly, Italian fascism rejected the Marxist view of the class struggle, preferring a sort of class collaboration that reaffirmed caste hierarchy with its attendant duties.[22] In this tradition, the Johnson County War represents the inevitable outcome of the corruption of hierarchy by installing the bourgeoisie economic caste as the political power.

The source of the range war conflicts stem in overloading the carrying capacity of the region: too many cattle mean that the grain is consumed with none left for winter, and their stomping crushes young seedlings; too many sheep means that the grass is eaten down to the roots and dies; blocking access to water limits possible grazing in that region because cows will need to constantly move out of it to find other sources. The early solution of massive, state-wide herds caused this problem because no one person had both the perspective to realize that the range was being overcrowded as well as the power to force herders to limit the number of cattle they owned. Moreover, the carrying capacity of the state varies widely based on the biome and weather: a 1000-lb cow and calf must graze between 10-50 acres in a bad year in the different parts of the state, but under optimal conditions they may only need 5-20 acres for the year.[23] However, to do so sustainably, they must graze over twice that area to allow for wild animals and reseeding. On the other hand, the failure of the legislature to firmly establish property rights in the region led to the problems mentioned above. The solution, which in fact took place, is to strictly separate cattle ranges so that each rancher can determine the optimum carrying capacity of their land, and by being near their cattle, they will know when additional food is required to survive droughts or winter storms.

However understood, the prevailing circumstances in Wyoming at the close of the 19th century reflected a growing contradictions between the common practice of prior appropriation of public land, to the exclusion of competitors, the understanding of public land as a common resource, and the increasing use of federal land claims to secure prime homesteads that threatened to block water access to the herds of large cattlemen. Simultaneous with the litigation of land access in the public domain in the field of rifles and violence, the economic foundation of the cattle industry collapsed after the Big Die-Up. Foreign investment pulled out, herds were liquidated, and it soon became nearly impossible to secure a loan to expand a herd on credit.[7] These conditions certainly made the cattlemen more protective of their dwindling profits and provided an incentive to divert blame onto criminal actors on the range. By doing so, they legitimized the practice of marginalizing the "criminal actors", appropriating their wealth, and using violence to ensure compliance.

Through this understanding, the Johnson County War, and the range wars which were contemporary with it, are an understandable response to the looming existential crisis for the distribution of scarce resources. The range wars represent the accretion of a secular modernity pulled between the yeomanism of the Jefferson era and the corporate concentration of the Gilded Age. While federal policy at the time favored small claimants, the history of economic development has favored the self-amplifying nature of capital. In the absence of a lawmaker to decide these conflicts, as was the case on the frontier, force is judge, and bloodshed the jury. The cattle barons may not have won the Johnson County War, but it is not clear that they lost.

~

The best original source on the Johnson County War is Asa Shinn Mercer's *The Banditti of the Plains*, which was originally written in 1894 and reprinted by the University of Oklahoma Press, and forms the backbone of most modern accounts.[7] Much of Mercer's account of the activities of the cattlemen's posse comes from the confession of George Dunning, a hired gun from Idaho, whose 44 page confession is reproduced in an appendix of *The Banditti of the Plains* and whose original resurfaced in 1961, apparently in a private collection.[24] Helena Huntington Smith's 1966 book, *The War on Powder River*, vacillates between castigating the cattlemen and the "rustlers" of Johnson County, and contains much more analysis of the characters involved, the historical background, and references.[10] The most recent analysis of this war is John Davis' *Wyoming Range War*, published in 2012, which incorporated administrative records and trial transcripts in his analysis.[14] The incident was extensively covered in local newspapers, but many are available only in physical archives.

Endnotes

1. Brown, M. H. *The Plainsmen of the Yellowstone*; G. P. Putnam's Sons: New York, 1961.
2. Morris, R. C. Map of Wyoming with Railroads. American Heritage Center, University of Wyoming: Laramie, Wyoming 1890.
3. Wyoming Stock Growers Association. *List of Members, by-Laws, and Reports of the Wyoming Stock Growers Association*; Bristol & Knabe Printing Co.: Cheyenne, Wyoming, 1887.
4. Jackson, W. T. The Wyoming Stock Growers' Association: Its Years of Temporary Decline, 1886-1890. *Agric. Hist.* **1948**, *22* (4), 260–270.
5. McFerrin, R.; Wills, D. High Noon on the Western Range: A Property Rights Analysis of the Johnson County War. *J. Econ. Hist.* **2007**, *67* (1), 69–92.
6. Eaton, J. W. The Wyoming Stock Growers Association's Treatment of Nonmember Cattlemen during the 1880s. *Agric. Hist.* **1984**, *58* (1), 70–80.
7. Mercer, A. S. *The Banditti of the Plains*, 1976th ed.; University of Oklahoma Press: Norman, Oklahoma, 1894.
8. Western, S. The Wyoming Cattle Boom, 1868-1886. *Wyoming History Encyclopedia*; Wyoming Historical Society, 2014.
9. Jackson, W. T. The Wyoming Stock Growers' Association Political Power in Wyoming Territory, 1873-1890. *Mississippi Val. Hist. Rev.* **1947**, *33* (4), 571–594.
10. Smith, H. H. *The War on Powder River*; University of Nebraska Press: Lincoln, Nebraska, 1967.
11. Witte, E. E. Early American Labor Cases. *Yale Law J.* **1926**, *35* (7), 825–837.
12. Tortious Interference with Contractual Relations in the Nineteenth Century: The Transformation of Property, Contract, and Tort. *Harv. Law Rev.* **1980**, *93* (7), 1510–1539.
13. Belgrad, D. "Power's Larger Meaning": The Johnson County War as Political Violence in an Environmental Context. *West. Hist. Q.* **2002**, *33* (2), 159–177.
14. Davis, J. W. Wyoming Range War: The Infamous Invasion of Johnson County; University of Oklahoma Press: Norman, Oklahoma, 2012.
15. Gould, L. L. Willis van Devanter and the Johnson County War. *Mont. Mag. West. Hist.* **1967**, *17* (4), 18–27.
16. "The Invaders" Johnson County Cattle War. American Heritage Center, University of Wyoming: Laramie, Wyoming 1892.
17. Gould, L. L. Francis E. Warren and the Johnson County War. *Ariz. West* **1967**, *9* (2), 131–142.
18. David, R. B. The United States Army in the Aftermath of the Johnson County Invasion. *Ann. Wyoming* **1966**, *38* (1), 59–75.

19. Schubert, F. N. The Suggs Affray: The Black Cavalry in the Johnson County War. *West. Hist. Q.* **1973**, *4* (1), 57–68.
20. Chomsky, N. Class War: The Attack on Working People. *South. Humanit. Rev.* **1996**, *30* (1), 1–18.
21. Evola, J. *Metaphysics of War*, 3rd ed.; Arktos Media Ltd.: United Kingdom, 2011.
22. Mussolini, B. *The Doctrine of Fascism*, Reprint.; World Future Fund: Alexandria, Virginia, 1932.
23. Sebade, B. *Grazing Livestock on Small Acreages*; Laramie, Wyoming, 2016.
24. Smith, H. H. George Dunning: Mystery Man of the Johnson Co. Invasion. *Mont. Mag. West. Hist.* **1963**, *13* (4), 41–49.

About the Author:

Peter Iversen is a writer interested in the ways that peoples and nations grow, struggle to thrive, and disappear.

Follow him on Twitter: @Pete_Iversen

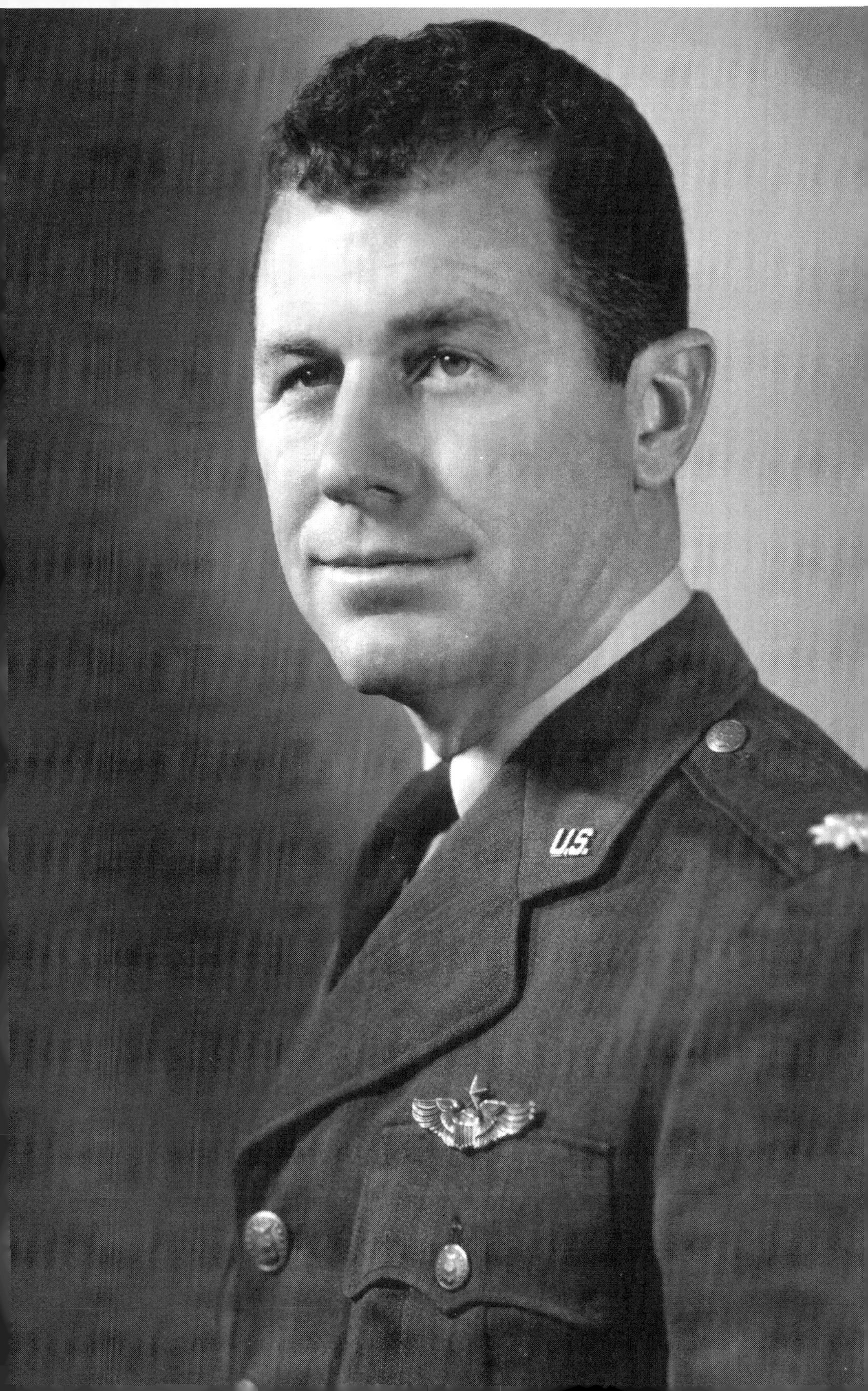
U.S.

Chuck Yeager:

The Man Who Unlocked the Stars

By Warriors of Old

> *"And finally, after the harsh test of calling upon all one's self-discipline, the feeling of an indescribable liberation, of a solar solitude and of silence; the end of the struggle, the subjugation of fears, and the revelation of a limitless horizon, for miles and miles while everything else lies down below – in all of this one can truly find the real possibility of purification, of awakening, of the rebirth of something transcendent."* [1]

Julius Evola is describing the feeling of summiting a mountain, yet his words seem even more aptly applied to an experience that only a very select few can claim – that of breaking out of the earth's atmosphere, of touching the sky.

Chuck Yeager was one of the first to experience that feeling of transcendence, as he sped past Mach 1 into the upper atmosphere of earth and looked out at the stars. He was so high, in such an ocean of space, that he couldn't even tell that he was moving.

He had touched the ceiling of the Earth.

Yeager was a pioneer in a long line of gutsy test pilots that opened up space as a new frontier for men to explore. His feats proved that men could break through not only the sonic barrier, but the atmospheric barrier.

Chuck Yeager was one of those men that would have gone unknown outside of certain aerospace and fighter pilot circles if it was not for the curiosity of Tom Wolfe and his classic book on rocket pilots, *The Right Stuff*. Thanks to Wolfe, Yeager's legend has grown in recent years. He was a country boy raised on the banks of the Mud River in Hamlin, West Virginia who spent his days hunting vermin and serving them up for family meals. Once he had graduated high school in September 1941, he enlisted in the Army Air Forces as a plane mechanic, but didn't take too much liking to the menial tasks involved. By July 1942 he had applied to join a flight program for enlisted men. When asked what made him want to be a pilot he replied simply: "I was in maintenance, saw pilots had beautiful girls on their arms, didn't have dirty hands, so I applied."[2]

From that moment on Yeager would go on to distinguish himself as possibly the gutsiest, most skilled pilot in that fabled fraternity of airborne daredevils. At the age of twenty, he was sent to Europe for his first taste of combat. In the words of Tom Wolfe, he "took off the feed-store overalls and put on a uniform and climbed into an airplane and lit up the skies over Europe."[3] He shot down two German fighters in his first eight missions, and on his ninth was shot down himself over German-occupied France. He bailed out and was picked up by the French underground, then smuggled into Spain disguised as a peasant. This is where Yeager showed that indomitable Appalachian spirit, a toughness that didn't even consider quitting as an option. Most downed pilots wouldn't return to combat, but Yeager was itching for a fight. On October 12, 1944, he shot down five German planes in a single mission, achieving in one day what most fighter pilots spent a career chasing: the title of ace. By the end of the war, then-22-year old Yeager had thirteen and a half kills under his belt.

Yeager's exploits in the war set the stage for his career as a test pilot. He went through test pilot training at Dayton's Wright Field in 1946 and 1947, and was then selected to go to Muroc Field in California for the XS-1 project, the backdrop for his greatest exploits. Muroc itself was a run-down airstrip in the middle of the Mojave Desert, unknown by most – but perfect for testing airplanes, with its flat, dried-up lake beds. Wolfe says: "Muroc seemed like an outpost on the dome of the world, open only to a righteous few, closed off to the rest of humanity [...] But to pilots this prehistoric throwback of an airfield became…shrimp heaven! The rat shack plains of Olympus!"[4]

Yeager was there to break the official rocket-plane speed record, which required flying faster than Mach 1 – the speed of sound. Mach 1 had developed a kind of mystique around it at this time. Attempts to reach it had run up against all kinds of weird phenomena: broken wind tunnels, locked-up controls, buffeting that could tear a plane apart. Just the year before, a British pilot named Geoffrey de Havilland tried to take a plane designed by his father to Mach 1, but the plane encountered so much buffeting that it was torn to pieces – along with de Havilland. For these reasons, many engineers and pilots didn't believe it could be done, referring to Mach 1 as the "sound barrier." This was the challenge facing the pilots and engineers at Muroc. They would be pushing man and machine to the limits of physics, hoping that both could take off and return to earth intact. These were men living – and dying – to "push the outside of the envelope." They possessed a quality – "the right stuff" – that enabled them to do the things that no one else thought possible, without even blinking an eye.

"It seemed to be nothing less than *manhood* itself [...] *Manliness, manhood, manly courage…* there was something ancient, primordial, irresistible about the challenge of this stuff, no matter what a sophisticated and rational age one might think he lived in."[5] Yeager embodied that quality, along with the rest of those "Knights of the Right Stuff" – and possibly more than most of them.

On October 14, 1947, the time came for him to put this quality on display – to break Mach 1. However, two nights before, Yeager had managed to break several ribs in a drunken horse-riding accident. On the morning of the flight, when he met with his flight engineer and fellow pilot Jack Ridley, the sullen Yeager informed him that, while he could surely tough it out for the flight, the pain was too much for him to lift his right arm up and secure the hatch of the X-1 Bell. This was problematic because the X-1 was launched in midair, from the belly of a B-29 bomber, and there wasn't enough room for him to get his left arm up to close the hatch.

Ridley, like some embodiment of Athena there to usher Yeager onto his heroic fate, came up with a plan involving a nine-inch piece of broom handle. Theoretically, there was just enough space for Yeager to reach up with his left arm and wedge the broomstick between the door and the handle, so he could close the door with the leverage of the stick.

Armed with a broomstick and the "most righteous stuff", Yeager descended into the X-1, whanged the door shut and took off straight into the sun. The X-1 climbed towards the heavens, and the machometer followed suit, reaching .87 Mach. Intense buffeting immediately followed – described over the radio by Yeager as "jes' the usual instability".

At .96 Mach, the X-1 regained stability, and eventually the needle on the machometer traveled off the scale altogether. It was then that the observers heard that legendary *boom*, resounding across the desert floor. Yeager had topped out at Mach 1.05, and, running out of fuel, was now staring out at the curvature of the earth – unable to tell that he was even moving as he looked into the ocean of space.

At that moment, Yeager opened a new frontier. He showed that both man and machine could withstand the speeds necessary to propel someone into earth orbit, and laid out the gauntlet for the legendary Mercury Seven that would be the first Americans to reach that goal. However, when describing the moment in his memoir, Yeager was actually underwhelmed:

> "It took a damned instrument meter to tell me what I'd done. After all the anticipation to achieve this moment, it really was a letdown. There should've been a bump in the road, something to let you know that you had just punched a nice, clean hole through the sonic barrier. The Unknown was a poke through Jell-O. Later on, I realized that this mission had to end in a letdown because the real barrier wasn't in the sky but in our knowledge and experience of supersonic flight."[6]

Yeager wanted it to be more difficult! This was the type of thumos he possessed. The man was a true warrior, with an insatiable hunger for adversity. In many ways, Yeager was the Achilles of space flight; much in the same way that the legend of Achilles inspired Alexander the Great, and Alexander inspired Julius Caesar, so too did the legend of Chuck Yeager challenge up-and-coming test pilots. The world of aviation in the late 40's and 50's was one of the fiercest meritocracies a person could find. Wolfe describes it as a ziggurat, with levels made up of every achievement and Yeager sitting at the top. So fierce was the fight to the top that many pilots would end up dying with their malfunctioning aircrafts, rather than ejecting and admitting they couldn't figure the problem out.

It was this spirit that led aviators to challenge Yeager's achievements with some of their own. Pilots like Neil Armstrong looked at what Yeager did and thought to themselves, "I can do better". That is what truly makes him a pioneer. He may not have been the first man into space proper, but he was the man who showed the world what could be done, just as Roger Bannister did when he ran a sub-four-minute mile. Yeager unlocked the stars.

~

Chuck Yeager represents a spirit that has vanished in the West, a spirit of exploration and adventure. He was just one of many such men, who reveled in the act of pushing themselves and their machines to limits that would likely end in death. Institutions like the Air Force and NASA used to be playgrounds for such young men; now, they languish in a mess of wokeism.

One of the most obvious losses when comparing Yeager's time to now is the loss of political will. While it is obvious that there were other factors that motivated the political will to conquer space – the motivation to beat the Soviets – the underlying attitude was nonetheless that of great men and a great nation, embarking on a journey of single-minded determination to overcome a great force: gravity. Such a goal brought out the best in a country that needed a strong purpose. John F. Kennedy said it best in his famous speech at Rice University:

> "We choose to go to the Moon. We choose to go to the Moon... We choose to go to the Moon in this decade and do the other things, not because they are easy, but because they are hard; because that goal will serve to organize and measure the best of our energies and skills, because that challenge is one that we are willing to accept, one we are unwilling to postpone, and one we intend to win, and the others, too."[7]

Compare that sense of energy to the present, and our current lack of skyward gaze is blatantly obvious. Political will is now so driven towards ideological ends that no heroes can remain. A Yeager-like character could never exist today, because he is too genuine. He was just a pilot that wanted to fly high and fast. Today, that's not enough. A modern Yeager would have to affix a pride flag to his test plane, and talk about his daily struggles with anxiety on CNN. This type of phenomenon is clear when observing how the media treats men like Elon Musk, someone who is reaching for the stars despite the lack of political will – only because he has the resources to do so. Even in the case of Elon, the ideology seeps in.

It is possible that a great project like the Mercury and Apollo programs could revitalize the West. But even if not, men like Chuck Yeager still deserve to be remembered, to be held up as the pioneers that they were.

The Greeks had a word, *arete*, that describes someone or something that has realized their full potential or degree of excellence. Yeager exhibited this arete in his mastery of the skies.

If nothing else, he should be remembered for that.

Endnotes

1. Evola, Julius. *Meditations on the Peaks: Mountain Climbing as Metaphor for the Spiritual Quest* (Rochester, VT: Inner Traditions) 2000, p.14
2. Yeager, Chuck. Twitter Post. September 3, 2016, 12:01 PM https://twitter.com/GenChuckYeager/status/772102166538428416
3. Wolfe, Tom. *The Right Stuff* (New York: Picador) 1979, p.35
4. Ibid, p.37-38
5. Ibid, p.21
6. Yeager, Chuck. *Yeager: An Autobiography* (New York: Bantam Books) 1985, p. 200
7. John, Kennedy. "Address at Rice University on the Nation's Space Effort" (speech, Houston, TX, September 12, 1962), NASA, https://web.archive.org/web/20180315230845/https://er.jsc.nasa.gov/seh/ricetalk.htm

About the Author:

Warriors of Old is a history enjoyer with interests in preserving the memories of great men.

Follow him on Twitter: @WarriorsOfOld

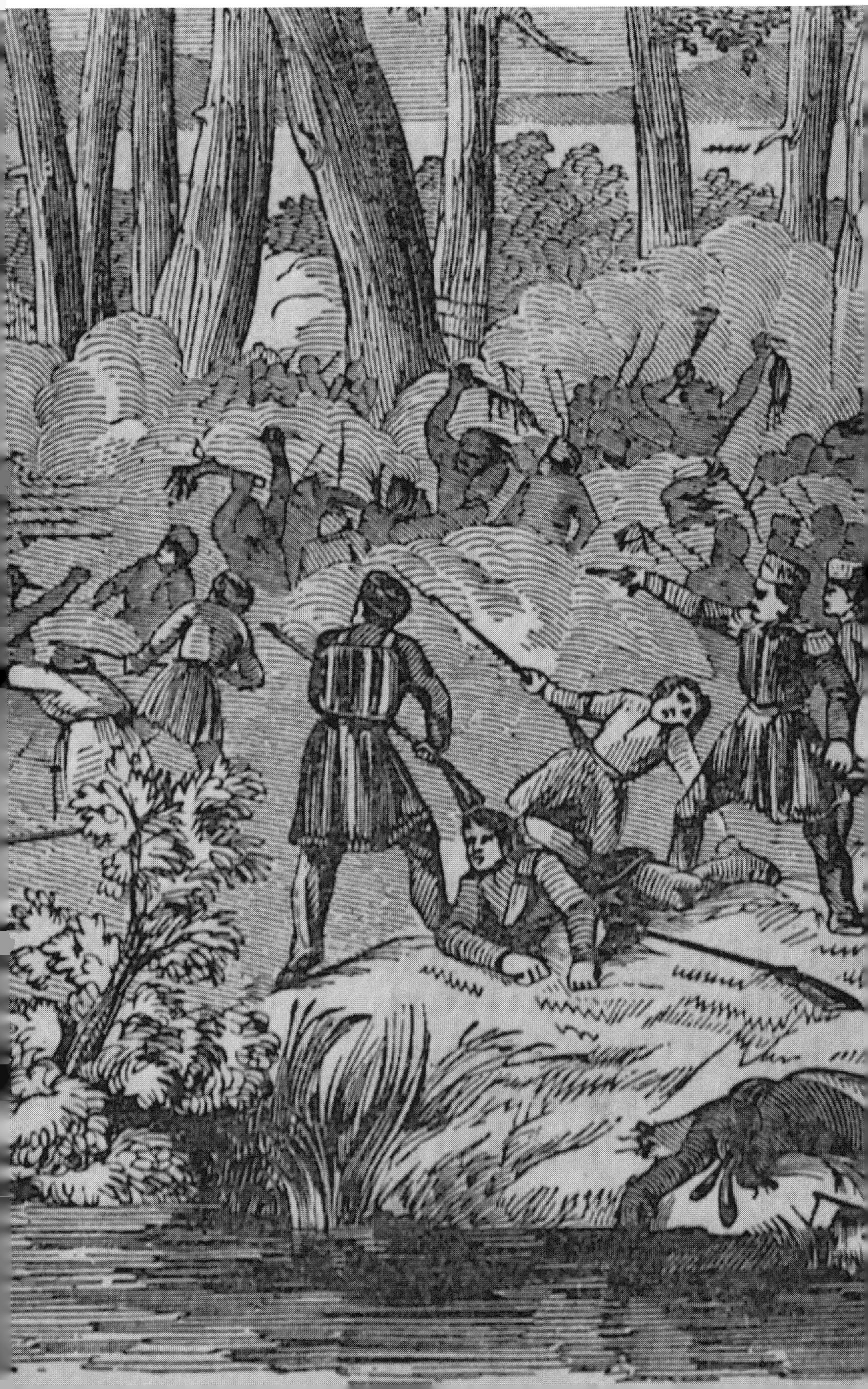

Cornstalk's Curse

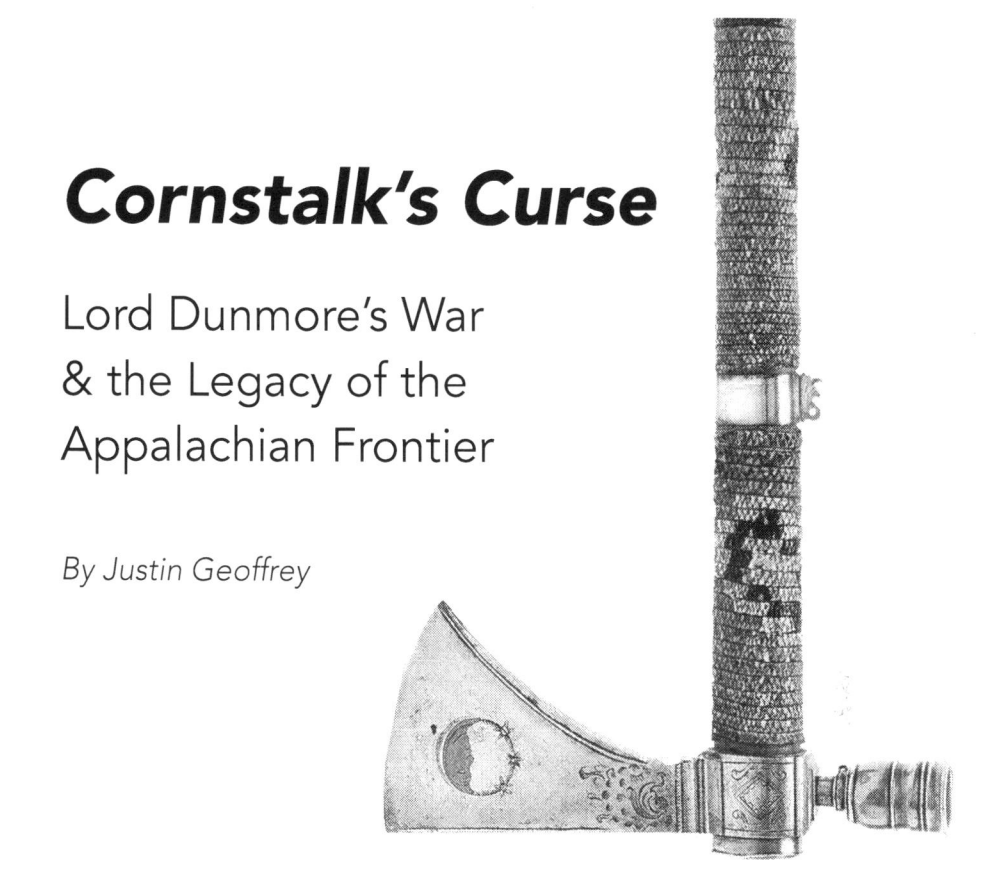

Lord Dunmore's War & the Legacy of the Appalachian Frontier

By Justin Geoffrey

During the early morning hours of October 10, 1774, between 800 and 1,100 warriors representing the Shawnee and Mingo tribes crossed the Ohio River. They traveled five miles upriver in canoes until they reached Old Town Creek. Here, the warriors camped and waited until dawn. At that point, the Shawnee and Mingo braves initiated battle against about one thousand Virginia militiamen from Augusta, Botetourt, Fincastle, and Culpepper counties. These hardy backwoodsmen, dressed and armed at their own expense, would soon find themselves fighting for survival at a piece of land along the Ohio that one of their own, Simon Kenton, dubbed "Point Pleasant."[1] Unbeknownst to all participants, their actions that day would have profound ramifications across multiple frontiers, including the invisible one of spirits, omens, and curses.

~

Britannia Rules the World

The Battle of Point Pleasant, which ended the brief conflict known as Lord Dunmore's War of 1774, had its origins in an earlier and much deadlier conflict. Known to Americans as the French and Indian War, the Seven Years' War (1756-1763) between Great Britain and France was one of the first true world wars that pitted competing colonial powers against one another. The heaviest fighting occurred in Europe and India. On the Continent, the Anglo-Prussian coalition scored major victories at Prague, Krefeld, and Freiberg. The Protestant ascendancy (plus British-aligned Russia and Portugal) of London and Berlin changed the balance of power in Central and Eastern Europe by weakening the traditional Catholic forces of France and Austria. However, although the war soaked Europe's fields with claret, the real meat was consumed out in the periphery of European power. In India, where the mighty Mughal Empire fought to maintain its hegemony over the Subcontinent, the East India Company and her Indian and Portuguese allies nearly erased all vestiges of French power and influence.[2] The hero of the hour for the British was Robert Clive, a former clerk in the East India Company's civil service at Madras. Despite his lack of prior military experience, Clive managed to make rank as a brevet captain in 1751.[3] Efficient, melancholic, and determined to make British control of India complete, Clive oversaw the immaculate success at Plassey, wherein a small Anlo-Indian force of 1,000 Europeans and 2,100 native troops armed with 100 gunners and eight cannons routed a Franco-Indian army that included 35,000 infantrymen and 15,000 in cavalry.[4] Clive's men used their cannons to repulse human wave attacks ordered by Suraj-ud-Daula, and although the French used artillery of their own, Clive's decision to screen his men behind a hill proved wise. Ultimately, the British lost a mere twenty-three killed and forty-nine wounded in comparison to Suraj-ud-Daula's force, which lost one out of every fifteen soldiers to death or injury.[5]

The victory at Plassey resulted in the British conquest of Bengal, which in turn meant that most of the Subcontinent was either directly or indirectly controlled by the powerful East India Company. The victory propelled Clive to the position of Governor of Bengal. Under Clive's watch, Bengal became the wealthiest province under Company control. The bureaucratic administration expanded, and much-needed military reforms turned the province's military into something worthy of comparison with the best forces in Europe. However, at each step of the way, Clive was accused of corruption and plundering by his political enemies in Britain. The chorus of jeers grew so loud that, on November 24, 1774, Clive took his own life. He died with a tarnished name, but a personal fortune worth 33 million pounds in today's money.[6]

The British success in India mirrored their success in North America. The Plassey of the Western Hemisphere took place on September 13, 1759, on the Plains of Abraham in Quebec City. Here, 4,400 British regulars and colonial rangers mostly from New England marched on Quebec against a French force that mixed French Army regulars with Quebecois militia and native warriors representing such fearsome tribes as the Mi'kmaq and Abenaki. Successful British volleys, alongside Royal Navy support, "shredded the French lines" within half an hour.[7] A new martyr, Major General James Wolfe, whom French sniper fire struck in the wrist, abdomen, and chest,[8] was born at the precise moment of his death. From that point on, the eastern half of North America came under the sole authority of Anglo-American civilization, where it remains today, however unstable or challenged. Yet, the British response to their victory in the Seven Years' War created a new conflict—an intra-ethnic conflict between the British metropole and her American subjects.

The Appalachian Frontier is Born

Defeating the French and their allies cost the British Empire greatly. The National Debt increased from £74 million to £133 million.[9] To recoup their losses, pay off their debts, and secure control over the transatlantic trade between the American colonies and the motherland, Parliament began passing a slew of new taxes, some of which, including the taxes on tea and stamps, have become part of the American mythos. (Less remembered is the fact that American colonists in the 1760s and 1770s sought redress in royal authority, proclaiming to the crown that their royal charters meant that they were subjects of the king, not Parliament.[10]) The taxes were onerous, to be sure, but they were mostly suffered by the people of Boston, Philadelphia, and other mercantile centers where seaborne trade dominated the economy. For the rugged men in the hinterlands, especially in the Old Southwest, the Royal Proclamation of 1763 most stirred their hot blood to anger. Issued by King George III on October 7, 1763, the proclamation dictated that only the crown could legally purchase lands from the native tribes. Thus, all lands not yet owned by the crown belonged to the natives. The point of the decree was threefold: 1) to begin the process of assimilating the Francophone populations of New France who found themselves under British rule; 2) establish peaceful relations with the various tribes who lived beyond the Appalachian Mountains; and 3) bar the land-hungry American colonists from seeking further expansion. The British knew that American expansion west across the Appalachians would cause conflict with the tribes. Such conflicts cost money—money that London simply did not have. Thus, royal law declared the Appalachians as the furthest extent of Anglo-American civilization.[11]

The Royal Proclamation of 1763 proved that Britain did not understand her American subjects very well. The men who settled the rugged lands of western Virginia, southwestern Pennsylvania, and what would become Kentucky, Tennessee, and Ohio lived a "rural individualistic lifestyle supported by their belief in a strong, evangelical, protestant God and an equally intense distrust of any authority figure."[12] These men spoke the same tongue as the aristocrats of the Tidewater, but their culture and customs were vastly different. Scots-Irish Presbyterians and Englishmen from Northumberland joined Germans from the Rhineland to form the unique character of the Appalachian backcountry.[13] These men lived with their families on small farms that maintained strong distances from their nearest neighbors. They planted crops, hunted game, and lived a harsh lifestyle that combined wildness with extreme liberty. This culture of Appalachia is the germ that gave life to the Frontier Thesis of Frederick Jackson Turner, which argues that American democracy and American culture is derived solely from colonial expansion and the violent nation-building process it created.[14] And there was certainly a lot of violence.

Despite the Royal Proclamation, settlers continued to pour across the Appalachian Mountains, establishing cabins and trading posts all along the Ohio River. This expansion of white settlement displeased the area tribes, most notably the large and militant Shawnee. Tit-for-tat massacres of the type seen earlier in 17th century Massachusetts, Maine, and Virginia characterized life in this region throughout the mid-1700s. For example, in 1742, a band of twenty-eight Iroquois warriors, fresh from slaughtering Catawbas rivals in South Carolina, decimated all the cattle belonging to the white settlers along the James River in Augusta County. In response, some thirty-five settlers sought battle against the Iroquois on December 19, 1742. The battle, known to the Virginians as McDowell's Fight, ended in nineteen dead (eleven settlers and eight Iroquois).[15]

To avoid such violence, some settlers sought refuge in fortified blockhouses. Others left the area altogether and returned to more peaceful environs closer to the coast. Many stayed put and endured kidnapping raids and war parties. Sometimes these settlers enacted terrible vengeance, such as the Yellow Creek Massacre of April 1774. The Virginia settlers living in what is today Ohio County, West Virginia betrayed the Mingo leader

Logan by slaughtering and defiling the corpses of his family members, including the Mingo wife of a white settler.[16] This act, along with the fact that the chief perpetrators, the Greathouse brothers, escaped justice, drove Chief Logan to seek formal revenge. After failing to negotiate peace, the men in charge of the Miami, Ottawa, Mingo, Delaware, Wyndot, and Shawnee created an alliance to expel every white man, woman, and child from the Ohio River Valley.

War was born.

Lord Dunmore Moves Virginia West

While the tribes of the Ohio River Valley sharpened their hatchets and readied their rifles, the man nominally in charge of the white settlers cared more about gaining land than defending it. John Murray, 4th Earl of Dunmore had replaced William Nelson as the Governor of the Province of Virginia three years earlier in 1771. A former governor of New York and a known *bon vivant* with a habit of wearing kilts, Lord Dunmore fit in easily with the patricians of Williamsburg. He sent his three sons to William & Mary, and his wife, the Lady Charlotte, was a fixture at well-attended dances.[17] Lord Dunmore was also something of a schemer. The Scotsman desired the fertile and abundant lands across the Ohio River, and as a result he allied himself with Virginia land surveyors interested in claiming new territory for their colony. The Virginians proved eager volunteers for their governor's settlement campaigns. The prosperous and populous colony even engaged in skirmishes with Pennsylvania to gain suzerainty over the Alleghenies and what would become Virginia's own colony in Kentucky.[18, i] By 1774, Murray had enough men and ambition to bring the fight against the Shawnee-led alliance.

A two-pronged offensive consisting of 2,500 Virginia militiamen was drawn up and implemented by May 1774. Lord Dunmore, an experienced soldier who served in the 3rd Regiment of the Foot Guards, led about 1,500 militiamen from Fort Pitt (today's Pittsburgh, Pennsylvania) down the Ohio until that river reached another, the Kanawha. Another division of Virginians followed the orders of General Andrew Lewis, who marched his rugged mountaineers overland through some of the toughest country in North America. The purpose was to overwhelm tribal villages and force them into submission. And Dunmore marched right alongside his men as they wound down the serpentine route.[19]

By that September, most of Lord Dunmore's army made camp at an area of the Greenbrier River soon to be christened as

Camp Union (today's Lewisburg, West Virginia). Here, the Virginians resupplied themselves with food and ammunition sent over the mountains from Staunton. When fully stocked, Lord Dunmore's army split off into several factions once again, with the Augusta Regiment under Colonel Charles Lewis providing the spearpoint.[20] By the end of September, every Virginia rifleman had made it to the Elk River. Some records articulate that the men were restless; others speak of a general malaise of sadness that beat down the usually hardy frontiersmen. These feelings of trepidation most likely stemmed from the Shawnee and Mingo skirmishers who trailed the Virginians every step of the way. Rather than directly engage, these braves stayed in the shadows, and thus may have contributed to the feelings of unease experienced by the more keen-witted white militiamen. The Shawnee waited and kept their knives sharp. Fate sealed the two sides to battle when, in late September, Lord Dunmore ordered Lewis to proceed to Point Pleasant while he sought a higher position somewhere upriver. Sometime during this period, the lines of communication broke down between Dunmore and Lewis. Lewis's militiamen carried on alone without support from Dunmore's force. They made camp, established a blockhouse and cattle pens, and even made a makeshift church at Point Pleasant. The prevailing idea was that they would continue westwards. Chief Cornstalk had another idea.

Battle is Born

When Cornstalk's Shawnee and Mingo warriors crossed the Ohio and opened fire on the Virginia encampment, the militiamen initially believed that their opponents represented merely a scouting party. When they realized that their enemies were greater in number, the men from Botetourt County moved forward to the edge of the Ohio River, while Augusta County riflemen moved in parallel along one of the flanks. These movements were checked by the Shawnee, who used rifles procured from French traders to suppress the Virginians. A heavy fog descended over the cloying battlefield. At some point, it must have looked like shadows firing at one another. However, even the thickest fog could not obscure the fact that the Shawnee and Virginians got so close that they engaged in hand-to-hand fighting, with hatchets, knives, and rifle butts acquiring casualties on both sides. One of the first Virginians to fall was Joseph Hughey, who died at the hands of Tavender Ross, a white renegade who fought alongside the Shawnee.[21] Such men existed all across the Appalachian frontier in 1774, and indeed the threat posed by whites "gone native" was first articulated by the New Englander Mary Rowlandson, who witnessed some of her neighbors participating in the Narragansett raid on the frontier village of Lancaster, Massachusetts in February 1676.[22]

Officers were not spared death, either. Thanks to his red waistcoat, Colonel Charles Lewis made for an easy target. Struck in the lower abdomen, Colonel Lewis was heard to cry, "I am wounded but go on and be brave" as he was removed from the battlefield. Colonel Fleming of the Botetourt Regiment stayed in the fight until two rounds struck him in the chest and arm. Fleming walked to the rear under his own power.[23] These losses among the small officer corps almost turned the tide of the battle. Thankfully for the Virginians, Colonel Field's timely deployment of two hundred reinforcements from Culpepper County stabilized the Virginia lines. While his men saved the day, Colonel Field himself could not be saved. A Shawnee round struck Field in the head, killing him instantly.

The battle that day devolved into a million private wars, with the militiamen taking cover behind boulders and stumps to take aim at the equally atomized Shawnee and Mingo braves. Lines became unconnected and at times unwieldy. However, they existed, and General Andrew Lewis dispatched three captains—Isaac Shelby, George Matthews, and John Stuart—with orders to flank the enemy lines when and where possible. Also mobilized were scouts under the command of Colonel William Christian of Fincastle County. The savvy Cornstalk became aware of these flanking maneuvers as the morning gave way to the afternoon. He selected his best fighters, including his brother Silverheels and sister Nonhelema (nicknamed the "Grenadier Squaw" for her size and strength), to continue the fight until all the Shawnee dead and wounded could be pulled from the field. By nightfall, the Shawnee and Mingo dead belonged to the Ohio River, while the wounded Silverheels and others managed to safely cross to the other side.[24] The Virginians maintained their positions and managed to build some breastworks made from logs. They won the day, but it had come at a cost. A full twenty percent of the Virginian force was lost to either death or injury.[25] Many of the wounded lived out the remainder of their lives as invalids in the care of their impoverished families. One of the dead, Richard Trotter of Staunton, left behind a wife. Ann Trotter, originally an indentured servant from Liverpool, England, vowed revenge. Known later as "Mad Ann" and "the white squaw of Kanawha," the aggrieved widow became one of the legendary scouts, spies, and Indian fighters of the Old Southwest.

As for the principal players, Lord Dunmore and Cornstalk, they met on October 19, 1774, at a hastily erected campsite known as Camp Charlotte. The Virginians convinced the Shawnee leader to sign the Treaty of Camp Charlotte. The treaty ended the brief war when the Shawnee and Mingo agreed to abandon their hunting lands south of the Ohio River. Cornstalk also agreed to halt all attacks on white settlers in the area.[26] Conspicuous in his absence was Chief Logan. Logan did agree to the peace negotiations but refused to end his war against the

Americans. Using Simon Girty, a kidnapped settler raised among the Cayuga, as his messenger, Logan delivered one of the most famous speeches of the frontier. Known as "Logan's Lament," this piece of oratory would later be lionized by Thomas Jefferson as one of the founding pieces of Virginian literature:

> "I appeal to any white man to say, if he ever entered Logan's cabin hungry, and he gave him not meat; if he ever came cold and naked, and he cloathed [sic] him not. During the course of the last long and bloody war Logan remained idle in his cabin, an advocate for peace. Such was my love for the whites, that my countrymen pointed as they passed, and said, 'Logan is the friend of white men.' I had even thought to have lived with you, but for the injuries of one man. Colonel Cresap,[ii] the last spring, in cold blood, and unprovoked, murdered all the relations of Logan, not even sparing my women and children. There runs not a drop of my blood in the veins of any living creature. This called on me for revenge. I have sought it; I have killed many; I have fully glutted my vengeance; for my country I rejoice at the beams of peace. But do not harbour [sic] a thought that mine is the joy of fear. Logan never felt fear. He will not turn on his heel to save his life. Who is there to mourn for Logan?-Not one."[27]

Chief Logan would continue to bedevil white settlers in the Ohio Country until his death in 1780. During the American Revolution, he allied himself with the pro-British Mohawk and ordered deadly raids on American settlements. These raids would claim many lives, especially among the frontier settlements in Pennsylvania and western Virginia. And while Logan died peacefully and in obscurity, the spirit of revenge that he set in motion following the Yellow Creek Massacre would not end until the Battle of Fallen Timbers in 1794. At that conflagration, Major General "Mad" Anthony Wayne and about 3,000 members of the American Legion (the successor to the Continental Army) squared off against Chief Blue Jacket, a Shawnee veteran of Point Pleasant.[28] Wayne's victory at Fallen Timbers finally secured the Alleghenies and Appalachians for the Americans by not only forcing the Shawnee and allied tribes like the Miami, Ojibwa, and Wyandot to move further north and west to avoid the growing American population in the Ohio and Indiana territories, but the victory also convinced the British, who still garrisoned forts all across the Midwest and Lower Canada, to seek a new peace with the Early Republic.[iii] Thus, Fallen Timbers was the final battle of a war that began with the Battle of Point Pleasant.

Cornstalk's Curse

Many of the veterans of Point Pleasant would go on to play significant roles in the American Revolution. Captain George Matthews would later serve as a brevet general in the Continental Army before transitioning to civilian politics. The latter role would see Matthews as the Member of the U.S. House of Representatives for Georgia's Third District (1789-1791) and the Governor of Georgia (1793-1796). Another veteran of the campaign, Daniel Morgan, would lead one of the first Virginia companies of the Revolutionary War. Morgan's riflemen, known as "Morgan's Sharpshooters," proved their elite status time and time again during pivotal battles at Saratoga and Cowpens.[29] As for Colonel John Field of Culpepper County, his greatest legacy was genetic. From his line came the Bush family that produced two presidents.[30] One of the fallen on the native side was none other than the father of Tecumseh, the Shawnee chief who brought death and destruction to the American settlements of the Midwest during the War of 1812.[31]

But what of the battle's two leaders—Lord Dunmore and Cornstalk? The war that ended in 1774 was merely a prelude to the war that began in 1775. Lord Dunmore remained the Virginia governor at the outbreak of the American Revolution. The arch-Loyalist Dunmore fled the Governor's Mansion at Williamsburg on June 7, 1775. Still proclaiming himself as the rightful ruler of Virginia, Dunmore created an army whilst living aboard the Royal Navy ship HMS *Fowey* as it anchored outside of Yorktown. It was here that Dunmore devised a scheme to damage the Virginia Patriots militarily and economically. He invoked his authority as the crown's representative in Virginia to offer freedom to any slave willing to serve in the British Army or a Loyalist militia.[32] Dunmore's army of runaway slaves was christened as the Ethiopian Regiment. Under the banner of "Liberty to Slaves," the regiment fought two battles—Kemp's Landing and Great Bridge. The regiment was disbanded following their defeat at Great Bridge and relocation to Staten Island in 1776. At that time, Dunmore remained in Virginia at his headquarters on Gwynn's Island. Dunmore, the last royal governor of Virginia, would finally sail to England following a Patriot bombardment of his headquarters in July 1776. The man who fired many of those cannons was none other than Brigadier General Andrew Lewis, Dunmore's subordinate at Point Pleasant.[33] Dunmore died far away from Virginia at his home in Kent in 1809.

Chief Cornstalk did not live to see the end of the 1770s. In October 1777, Cornstalk was taken hostage after he and two other Shawnee leaders traveled to Fort Randolph in order to inform Captain Matthew Arbuckle, another Point Pleasant veteran, of illegal settlements in the Ohio Country.[34] By all accounts, Cornstalk was treated well in confinement until a white hunter was killed by either the Shawnee or Mingo near the Kanawha River on November 9th. An enraged mob broke into Fort Randolph and shot Cornstalk seven times.[35] Supposedly, just after the first shots entered his body, Cornstalk invoked the Great Spirit to place a curse on the land and the people of the Ohio River Valley.

The cold-blooded murder of Chief Cornstalk is believed by some to be the cause of what is known as The Cornstalk Curse. The first victim was Cornstalk's daughter Bluesky, who committed suicide upon hearing the news of her father's murder.[36] Other incidents blamed on the curse include things as varied as unusual lightning strikes to the 1907 Monongah Mine Disaster that killed 310 miners far away from the Ohio River in Marion County, West Virginia.[37] However, whenever the Cornstalk Curse is invoked, word invariably turns to Point Pleasant, West Virginia and the sudden appearance of the Mothman in 1966.

First sighted by gravediggers working in a Clendenin, West Virginia cemetery, the creature's best-known description came courtesy of a pair of young lovers who reported seeing a large monster with 10-foot wings and glowing red eyes that chased them out of a former munitions factory from the Second World

War.[38] Sightings suddenly erupted in and around Point Pleasant, with local residents identifying the creature as everything from an extraterrestrial to a demon. The terror ratcheted up until December 1967, when the Silver Bridge, which connected U.S. Route 35 over the Ohio River, collapsed due to stress fractures caused by heavy rush hour traffic. Forty-six people perished in the disaster.[39] Following the demise of the Silver Bridge, the Mothman disappeared from Point Pleasant. Was the cryptid a warning all along? Did its appearance portend the Silver Bridge tragedy? Many believe this, just as many believe that the Mothman and the Silver Bridge disaster are connected back to the dying words of the wrathful Chief Cornstalk. The Shawnee may have lost the battle in the material world, but did they score a victory in the spiritual realm?

Lord Dunmore's War and the Battle of Point Pleasant are often cosigned to the shadows of regional history. Those who know of these events at all consider them only informative or interesting to the residents of Ohio, West Virginia, and Kentucky. This is a tragic case of historical forgetfulness, for the events of 1774 not only set in motion the gradual conquest of the Old Southwest by American settlers (and thus led directly to the creation of the states of Ohio, Kentucky, and Tennessee), but they also proved the mettle of Virginia militiamen just in time for the larger war against Great Britain. Indeed, the same men who fought along the Ohio River in 1774 would later defeat Major Patrick Ferguson's superior force at King's Mountain in 1780. These Overmountain Men, although brutal and roughhewn, were the standard-bearers of a unique and easily identifiable American culture—the culture of the hillbilly, the Don't-Tread-on-Me individualist, the Appalachian mountaineer. This culture is still alive and in the same mountains where a long-dead Shawnee chief's curse may also linger. These two are forever entwined with the history of America's Appalachian region, which is itself part of the larger story of the Anglo conquest of North America.

Endnotes

1. James K. Swisher, "Lord Dunmore's War: The Battle of Point Pleasant," *Warfare History Network*, Web. Accessed 8 Apr. 2023, <https://warfarehistorynetwork.com/lord-dunmores-war-the-battle-of-point-pleasant/>.
2. Fred Anderson, *Crucible of War: The Seven Years' War and the Fate of Empire in British North America*, 1754-1766 (New York and Toronto: First Vintage Books, 2001): 417.
3. "Robert Clive: The nabob general," *National Army Museum*, Web. Accessed 8 Apr. 2023, <https://www.nam.ac.uk/explore/robert-clive>.
4. Paul K. Davis, "Plassey," *100 Decisive Battles: From Ancient Times to the Present* (Oxford and New York: Oxford University Press, 2001): 240.
5. Davis, "Plassey," 243.
6. "Robert Clive: The nabob general."
7. Paul K. Davis, "Quebec," *100 Decisive Battles: From Ancient Times to the Present* (Oxford and New York: Oxford University Press, 2001): 247.
8. Ibid.
9. "How Britain lost an empire – war and government," *BBC Bitesize*, Web. Accessed 8 Apr. 2023, <https://www.bbc.co.uk/bitesize/guides/zyh9ycw/revision/2#:~:text=In%20spite%20of%20the%20victory,and%20the%20%27mother%20country%27>.
10. Eric Nelson, *The Royalist Revolution: Monarchy and the American Founding* (Cambridge, MA and London: Harvard University Press, 2014): 95.
11. "Royal Proclamation of 1763," *The Canadian Encyclopedia*, 2019 Aug. 30. Web. Accessed 8 Apr. 2023. <https://www.thecanadianencyclopedia.ca/en/article/royal-proclamation-of-1763>.
12. Swisher, "Lord Dunmore's War."
13. David Hackett Fisher, *Albion's Seed: Four British Folkways in America* (Oxford and New York: Oxford University Press, 1989): 739.
14. Frederich J. Turner, "The Significance of the Frontier in American History," *Annual Report of the American Historical Association* (Chicago, 1893): 197-227.
15. Warren R. Hofstra, *The Planting of New Virginia: Settlement and Landscape in the Shenandoah Valley* (Baltimore & London: The Johns Hopkins University Press, 2004): 17.
16. Henry Howe, *Historical Collections of Ohio, Containing a Collection of the Most Interesting Facts, Traditions, Biographical Sketches, Anecdotes, Etc., Relating Its General and Local History: with Descriptions of Its Counties, Principal Towns and Villages* (Cincinnati: Derby, Bradley & Co., 1847): 267.
17. Swisher, "Lord Dunmore's War."

18. Bert Dunkerly, "The War on the Pennsylvania Frontier: Part 5 of 5: The war between Virginia and Pennsylvania," *Emerging Revolutionary War Era*, 2019 Dec. 23. Web. Accessed 9 Apr. 2023. <https://emergingrevolutionarywar.org/2019/12/23/the-war-on-the-pennsylvania-frontier-part-5-of-5-the-war-between-virginia-and-pennsylvania/>.
19. Swisher, "Lord Dunmore's War."
20. Ibid.
21. Ibid.
22. For more information, please see Rowlandson's autobiography, *Narrative of the Captivity and Restoration of Mrs. Mary Rowlandson*.
23. Swisher, "Lord Dunmore's War."
24. Ibid.
25. Ibid.
26. Ken Sullivan, "Treaty of Camp Charlotte," *The West Virginia Encyclopedia*, 2013 Dec. 23. Web. Accessed 9 Apr. 2023. < https://www.wvencyclopedia.org/articles/766>.
27. Qtd. In Thomas Jefferson, *Notes on the State of Virginia*, edited by William Peden (New York: W.W. Norton, 1954): 63.
28. Matthew Seelinger, "The Battle of Fallen Timbers, 20 August 1794," *Army Historical Foundation*, 16 Jul. 2014, Web. Accessed 9 Apr. 2023. https://armyhistory.org/the-battle-of-fallen-timbers-20-august-1794/.
29. John W. Wright, "The Rifle in the American Revolution," *American Historical Review*, Jan. 1924, Vol. 29, No. 2, 293-299.
30. William Addams Reitwiesner, "Ancestry of George W. Bush," Web. Accessed 9 Apr. 2023. <http://www.wargs.com/political/bush.html>.
31. R. David Edmunds, *Tecumseh and the Quest for Indian Leadership*, 2nd Ed. (New York: Pearson Longman, 2007): 16-18.
32. Kevin Phillips, *The Cousins' Wars: Religion, Politics, Civil Warfare, And The Triumph of Anglo-America* (New York: Basic Books, 1999): 221.
33. Swisher, "Lord Dunmore's War."
34. Ibid.
35. Ibid.
36. Fred O'Neill, "Cornstalk's curse and other area legends," *The Marietta Times*, 7 Jul. 2014. Web. Accessed 9 Apr. 2023. <https://www.mariettatimes.com/opinion/local-columns/2014/07/cornstalk-s-curse-and-other-area-legends/>.
37. Ibid.
38. Meghan Overdeep, "The Terrifying Tale of West Virginia's Legendary Specter: The Mothman," *Southern Living*, 26 Oct. 2022.
39. Ibid.

Additional Notes

i   The idea of a colony having its own vassal states is not entirely novel. Less than a century after Virginia began its independent administration of Kentucky, the Ottoman colony of Egypt independently administered Sudan.

ii As previously mentioned, the Yellow Creek Massacre that targeted Chief Logan's family was carried out by the Greathouse brothers, not Colonel Cresap. The reasons for this mistake are unknown, but Colonel Thomas Cresap was a settler-soldier who fought in a major border dispute between Maryland and Pennsylvania.

iii This was short-lived, as the later War of 1812 was caused in part by British agents fomenting further native attacks on White settlements in the Old Northwest.

About the Author:

Justin Geoffrey is a Canadian-born but American-raised alchemist, Christian mystic, NEET spiritualist, and writer.

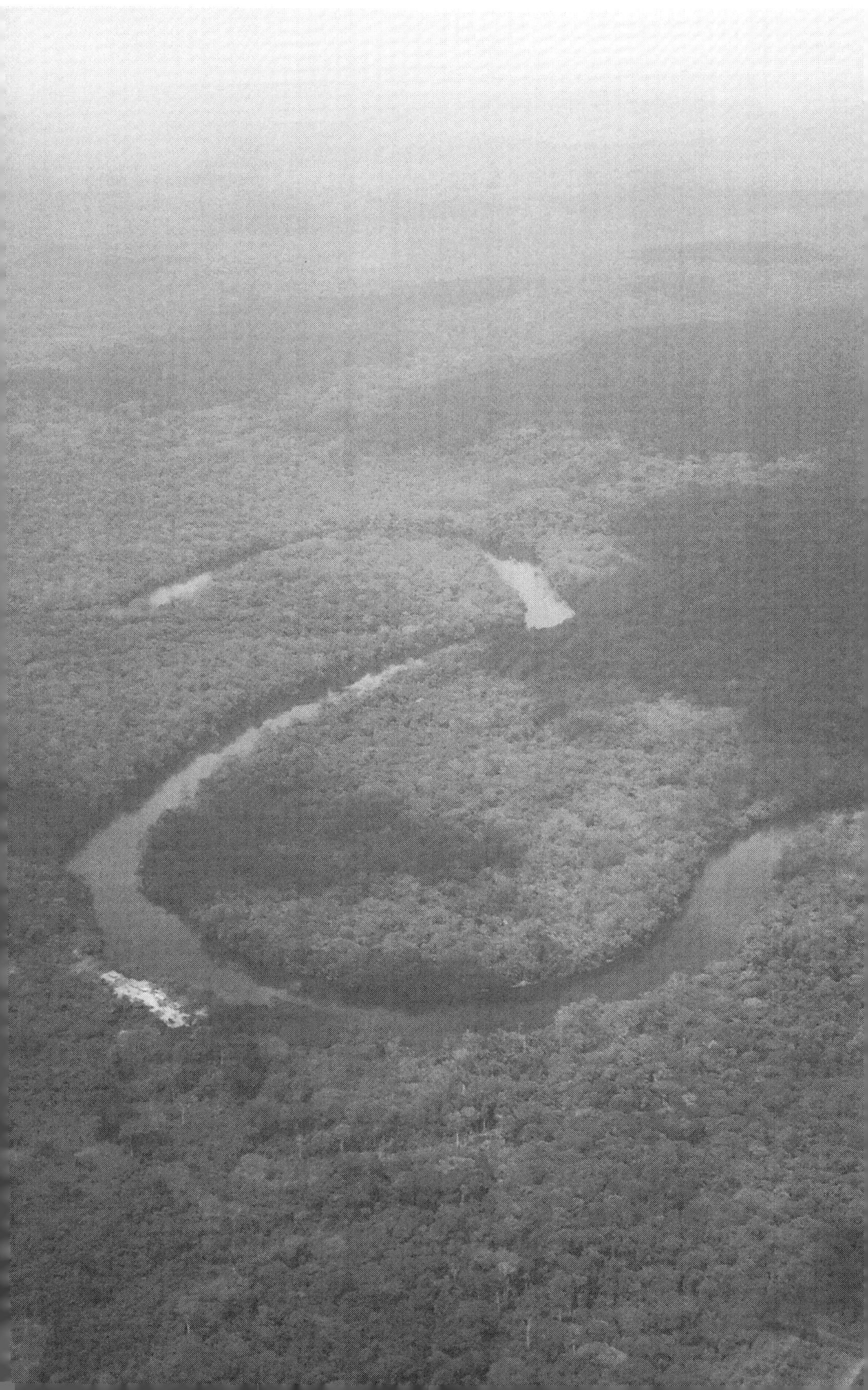

The Memoirs of Rafał Gan-Ganowicz

Translated by "Blue-Eyed Genghis"

Rafał Gan-Ganowicz (1932-2002) was a man with a single-minded, unrelenting sense of focus – a focus which for his entire life was centered on fighting communism.

As a child, he had lost both of his parents during the German invasion of Poland. Then, as a teenager he witnessed the atrocities of Soviet occupation; he was particularly affected by the wanton destruction wrought by the Soviets, as well as the meaningless violence. One instance that he often recalled involved Soviet soldiers throwing one of his friends – who had lost a leg in the Warsaw Uprising – down a flight of stairs, baselessly calling him a "bandit." During this time, he became involved in the anti-communist youth resistance movement, spray-painting slogans, interfering with propaganda efforts, and stealing guns from the police. However, in 1950 the Secret Police began closing in on him, and he was forced to leave the country for West Berlin.

There, due to his status as a political refugee, Ganowicz was able to join the Polish Guard of the US Army. He trained as a paratrooper, reaching Second Lieutenant, but was unsatisfied with mere patrols. He had hoped that the Polish Guard would lead an attack on the Soviet Union; when that failed to materialize, he left the Army and decided to fight communism on his own terms.

In the mid-1960s, the place to do this was Africa: where the US and the USSR met in a proxy war, deep in the jungles of the

Congo. Ganowicz volunteered for service at the Congolese embassy in Paris, and was soon leading men in this untamed land – contending with natives and nature utterly foreign to the First World.

Here, we have published selections from Ganowicz's memoirs regarding his time in the Congo. Translated for the first time into English, these passages provide an insight into that wild frontier, and the forgotten conflict that called to Rafał Gan-Ganowicz in his personal crusade against communism.

Today, Gan-Ganowicz is little-known in the West, except for a particular interview regarding his time in the Congo. Allegedly, a reporter asked him what it felt like to take human life. He responded: "I wouldn't know. I've only ever killed communists."

Dollars Get Greener in the Jungle

The brigade headquarters was located in the center of the city, on a wide avenue shaded by two rows of trees. By the time the check-in was over, it was late afternoon. Stepping out of the air-conditioned room of the briefing room into the sun-drenched courtyard, I unzipped my sweatshirt. After crossing the field, I felt the first drops of sweat running down my back. The day was unusually humid even for the climate of Stanleyville. I walked briskly toward the service jeep, dreaming of the cool breeze as I'd speed through the city at my usual pace. It was one of the prized perks of the job: a short honk of the horn, and the police stopped traffic with a polite salute when they saw me. I had left the Jeep in the shade under the trees. As I approached it, a figure jumped out from behind the bushes. I quickly drew my pistol and hid to the side: assassination attempts were frequent.

I felt a little ridiculous, recognizing Takarios' stout figure. Takarios was the spokesman for the Greek colony at Stanleyville. All trade here was in the hands of the Greeks. They made money quickly because they risked their lives for trade. They went with military patrols to the most vulnerable outposts and settlements. They took risks, bringing in goods often under fire. They were dying. But they were making a fortune. Takarios was their boss. He borrowed money and made deals with the authorities, gave bribes…

A moment later I was sitting in a Greek restaurant, in a separate office in the back, at a lavishly laid table. Takarios needed something. And since the army sometimes needed Greek merchants, it was worth listening to my interlocutor. Could he mean incorporating a few Greek merchants and their trucks to the nearest military supply transport?

Anyone who saw the march of the Red Army at the end of World War II will never forget the Soviet vandalism. What the Soviet could not steal, he destroyed. Soviet soldiers threw radios and gramophones out of the windows, bayoneted portraits, tore strings from pianos, smashed washbasins, and toilet bowls, shot at mirrors and chandeliers, destroyed libraries, smashed furniture, and tore curtains to shreds. Every house they had inhabited, even if only for a few days, needed a thorough renovation. Not to mention the dirt and stench they left behind. If the toilet bowls were broken… Why did they destroy so badly? Were they driven to envy that someone could live in conditions that they, citizens of the "progressive country", saw only in the cinema? Or was it because of the propaganda that constantly told them that outside the Soviets there was terrible exploitation and that therefore every decent apartment appeared to be a capitalist's dwelling? Or is it the nature of Soviet man, fueled by vodka like a car engine is fueled by gasoline? I don't know. But I remember Soviet barbarism…

The negroes are not vandals! The Negro, neither the "wild" one from the jungle, nor the "civilized" one from the city, consciously destroys anything. In the recaptured territories of the rebellion, I found houses, villas, and workshops. More than one villa was in a dilapidated state, but that was not due to deliberate vandalism. A Negro family, having taken a Belgian villa, simply did not know how to use the facilities and comforts. Most of the time there was no electricity or gas. The "revolutionaries" did not know how to turn on the power plants and generators… So, in the villa bonfires were lit in the middle of the living room, on the often-priceless parquet floor. Smoke getting in your eyes? Holes were made in the ceiling and roof. Then the rains did their thing…

I saw the blackened walls, the burnt floor, the stains… But to my amazement, the radio equipment, useful for nothing, due to the lack of electricity, remained in its place. Even the plates weren't broken. Great fine porcelain tableware - intact. Leaving this place, the "wild" Negroes did not destroy anything consciously, they did not break anything.

When we speak of "civilized" nations, this is worth thinking about.

Such thoughts were running through my head when, after a few days of fighting, I was visiting the so-called "new airport." In fact, the airport was just under construction. It began to be built shortly before the outbreak of the rebellion with loans obtained from various countries, mainly Western European nations. With a flanking maneuver I managed to force the rebels to retreat into the jungle. Now I went from hangar to hangar and was shocked by what wasn't there! Unpacked crates of computers, fully equipped workshops, radar equipment, typewriters, telex machines, electric motors and generators, kilometers of cable. Huge fuel tanks: gasoline and oil, which Stanleyville was so short of that even the army was rationing them. Bulldozers, excavators, tractors... A fortune! All in good condition, nothing damaged. Thousands of spare parts in original packaging.

I posted up guards.

Father M. was an extraordinary man. A forty-something monk, a Belgian missionary, with great personal courage, he had not only a soul full of dedication and Christian zeal, but also a head full of all kinds of wisdom, and a kind smile on his lips. Father M. knew Negro dialects, customs, and superstitions. I became very friendly with him. The service he rendered me with his knowledge of the terrain was invaluable. It was he who found out that in the jungle, several kilometers from our most advanced outpost, there is a large group of Negro families who had escaped from Stanleyville in their time. Now, unaccustomed to life in the jungle, exposed to hunger, sick from lack of salt, they would like to return. They even tried but were shot at by a rebel force encamped between them and the desired city.

Our main pacification task was to ensure that the civilian population returned to their homes and activities. If, according to Mao Zedong, the revolutionaries are to be among the civilian population "like fish in water", then our "little red fish" should be deprived of this water by getting the tribes and families who wanted to return to normal life out of their clutches.

I've been waiting for a similar opportunity. I had enough of the staff, conferences, dealing with logistics. So, I decided to launch an attack on the rebel camp. Permission was not easy to obtain: that was not the role of a battalion commander. But fat Lamouline had just left, and Bob Denard had taken over. The latter, being a swashbuckler himself, understood well the need to immerse himself in combat, in adventure, in risk.

Third day in the jungle. My detachment of four Europeans and sixty Katangese - was getting more and more bogged down in the tangled vegetation. The first kilometers we traveled smoothly along a path trodden by elephants. But the path twisted and had to be abandoned. We were led by a young black man, Father M's catechumen. It was he who made his way to Stanleyville and brought the news to the priest about the fate of civilians, including his family, in the jungle. The four Katangese went ahead, single file, the one up front cut a path with a machete. The air was saturated with moisture. Each kilometer was a few hours of breaking through. The third day was coming to an end. On the equator, night falls quickly, almost suddenly. You have to think about rest.

During the night, a Katangese sergeant woke me up. Although, according to our guide, it was still a long way to the rebel camp, a day's journey, the Katangese smelled smoke. You have to admit that black people have a great sense of smell. So, though neither of us Europeans felt anything, I called the alarm. We started sneaking through the jungle, breaking through the vegetation. Cutting the way with a machete was out of the question: the noise would have warned the enemy. Our guide explained to me that this was definitely not the camp to which he was leading us. But we have to check. After an hour of strenuous scrambling, we reached an opening. Twelve bamboo huts in a clearing; an extinguished bonfire. No guards. In one of the huts the faint glow of a torch. Then, nothing. The jungle clatters with the cries of monkeys. The short roar of some predator. The awakened birds protest. I separated twelve groups of three from my force. One per cabin. Flashlight in hand. On my command - jump. Running through the clearing. I'm running too. I kick in the bamboo barrier, now in the hut. "Hands up!" - I scream. Flashlight flash on their faces. I was shuddered with exhilaration. There were four people in the hut. People? No. More like apparitions from a nightmare. They dragged themselves out of their beds making barely articulate sounds. A face without noses, eyes without lids were obscured by fingerless hands. Animal terror on inhuman faces. I stepped back. I felt the hair on my head stand up. Monstrous figures lingered from their beds and, babbling unintelligibly, walking towards me despite the muzzle of a submachine gun aimed at them. For God's sake! These are the lepers! I came to my own senses, ashamed of my own fear. I saw my army running out from the other huts. I had come across a leper camp. The Stanleyville rebels had blown up the leprosarium and hospitals, so the lepers fled into the forest. There, chased away by arrows, they died alone of hunger and exhaustion. A horrible fate.

I retreated from the leper camp. The rest of the night passed quietly.

Four hundred people got out of the jungle. Women and children made up the vast majority of the group that Father M's young apprentice had brought into town after I had managed to break up the rebel force. The children were so exhausted that several of them died in the hospital. Jean Bernard, one of my soldiers, was evacuated to Europe, where he died during an operation trying to sew his torn intestines together. A burst from the Kalashnikov is a nasty thing.

I thought of Bernard while looking at the pile of money lying on the lavishly laid table, among the remnants of food.

"Is twenty not enough?" asks Takarios. "We'll give thirty!"

A third pack appears on the table, containing one hundred hundred-dollar bills. I collected the money and shoved it into the Greek's open collar of his sweaty shirt. He looked at me surprised. I pulled on my cap and left without a word, ostentatiously unbuckling the holster of my pistol. Takarios must have been furious, and an angry Greek can be dangerous. But I got to the jeep without incident. Thirty thousand dollars to keep the Katangese guards eagerly guarding the hangars of the "new airport"! Easy and safe. It was enough in the presence of witnesses to give the order to keep watch, but not to ensure that it was carried out. Knowing the Katangese, one could be sure that they would not stay awake but sleep – and not at the police station, but somewhere in the city, with the women.

I lost thirty thousand dollars and gained a new enemy. I reinforced the guard and ordered them to be inspected by European non-commissioned officers. That same night someone tried to enter the airport grounds. A short burst from a submachine gun was the final persuasion. The attempt was not repeated again.

Sometimes, when I have no money, I can see before my eyes a table covered with food scraps and three hundred green bills.

Fireworks without a Christmas Tree during New Year's Eve

The cunningly planned offensive of the Reds collapsed. After four hours of fighting, the remnants of the rebels retreated in disarray, leaving dead and wounded behind. The wounded crawled into the jungle to find shelter. Without rescue or help, they died from loss of blood. The poor, stupid victims of propaganda from their leaders, who told them nonsense about our alleged cruelty. We acquired loads of guns. In fact, after that New Year's Eve night, our enemy never regained their strength and fitness again, at least on my sector of the front. For it all started on New Year's Eve 1965.

In fact, already on Christmas Day, a hail of bullets from Soviet 60 mm mortars rained down on us. And that was when Father M., our friend and priest, spoke about peace between people. I made a wild fuss with Father M. about the fact that he came to our facility on a bicycle! Such inconsideration! 25 kilometers of road where there were almost daily ambushes.

"Are you crazy? Couldn't you radio an escort? Who takes such risks?"

"I'm not afraid of anything" the priest replied impudently "Because I have this," he said, pointing at the wooden cross hanging on his belt.

"And if that doesn't help," he added after a moment, "I still have this!" He opened the flaps of his white robe, revealing to our astonished eyes a huge magnum revolver. "And you bastards, I couldn't leave you on Christmas Eve without religious consolation!"

He ended the tirade.

That it was raining shells on the Christmas Eve was normal for Soviet "militant atheism." There was not much damage, because the shooters were poor, and the observers preferred to "keep their heads down." However, many chimpanzees died out in the jungle. Then it kind of died down, and we thought it was over. So, on New Year's Eve I allowed all the off duty to gather in the facility hall and celebrate the New Year with "food and drink." Of course, having first taken care of the state of emergency of those whom blind fate in the form of my character has assigned on duty...

Over the course of the evening, my company managed to get quite high and began to ask me to let them have fireworks at midnight. In fact, we had some light mortar rounds in our equipment, the kind that then fall by parachute and illuminate the surroundings with a sparkle of magnesia.

We also had a large amount of light ammunition for small arms and machine guns. There were also multi-colored signal rockets and a corresponding flare launcher in my possession. Blessed my weakness! After a few shots, I'm ashamed to admit – I allowed it.

There was a bang, a shot, a series of colorful beads from machine guns rained down. Colorful rocket bursts. And hanging over everything were bright lanterns of magnesium shot from the mortar shells! July 14th in Paris is a puppy! Carnival in Rio is a sucker! Our souls rejoiced. But very briefly. Because suddenly, with a crash and with a whistle the wild roars rang out: *"Muelele May."*

We fired in an instant. The foreground illuminated by the New Year's Eve fireworks was swarming with attackers. They cunningly approached us at night, hoping that the New Year's Eve libations would put our vigilance to sleep. And it could have ended tragically for us. I'm ashamed to admit it, but I hadn't considered that possibility. What the cunning ones didn't anticipate was our firework display! We saw them completely unintentionally. They thought they had been detected and attacked us ahead of time. The surprise was on our side. Oh man, what a hard time they got on that New Year's Eve. Providence watches over drunkards – or maybe it's the prayers of Father M.

The New Year has started well for us. Not for everyone. I had to punish a French sergeant named Alain Fabregon. This young soldier wanted to impress us with his courage and in the open space, in full light, he turned his back, took off his trousers and showed the enemy... where the sun doesn't shine. For this feat, I punished him with a ban from action for a week. Alain died much later in an ambush. He died faithfully fulfilling his duty as a soldier, without pranks, and sober.

The undisputed winner of this memorable battle was our supplier of "food and drink", senior sergeant Konopka. Konopka, an old man from the Foreign Legion, had joined my unit a few months earlier. I made him an auxiliary petty officer. I must have been in a good mood. Konopka turned out to be a brilliant schemer. He gave and took bribes. He could find "things that are nowhere to be found." In a country where even potatoes were imported by air, in the full African jungle we ate oysters and drank champagne on New Year's Eve. And later... fireworks. Those blessed fireworks!

Sergeant Konopka's merits were, of course, not limited to stomach matters. Thanks to this scheme-master, my unit was the best equipped in all of the Congo. Konopka could find everything. Unusual ammunition for old guns, car parts, gasoline, medicine, and thousands of other things needed to wage war in unbearable conditions. Konopka left the Congo alive, safe and sound. And also, with a lot of money. We never saw him again. But this master of private initiative did not die for sure. He was going to America. He's probably a millionaire.

Barbecue Fisherman

Father M. ran panting up the hill to my outpost, holding up his white gown in both hands. It was obvious from his face that something unusual must have happened. I watched him anxiously. For I knew this extraordinary missionary and knew that there were few things in Africa that could upset him. So, I went to meet him. He muttered to me that he didn't want to speak in front of people, and ran into our canteen bar, where he demanded a whiskey in a stern voice. I got even more worried. Not because he drank it in a gulp, he was a known drinker, but because he drank it before noon, which, as you know, gentlemen don't do, and Father M. was undoubtedly a gentleman. Wiping his mouth with a checkered handkerchief the size of a tablecloth for six, he dragged me to the corner.

"Listen, Condottieri," he began in a hushed whisper (he always called me Condottieri). "Listen, Condottieri, it's incredible. Crocodile people have appeared!" He told me in horror. "From what I knew crocodile people haven't been seen in the Congo since the 1920s!" He was clearly agitated.

It all began in the morning when the trucks arrived at the fishing village at the foot of the hill where my outpost was located. The trucks would take them to Stanleyville, under military escort... fish from the night's catch. It was a matter of great importance: the city was starving. The fishermen settled in my newly conquered and pacified lands at the foot of the Wanie Rukula outpost on the Lualaba River, they were able to catch up to three tons of fish in one night. This was a major contribution to feeding the population of Stanleyville, which was cut off from the rest of the world. However, this time, nothing. Not a single piece.

It looked like some strange collusion, that none of the fishermen had fish. They did not go fishing that night. Why? Their excuses varied, as if they had something to hide: "My canoe cracked," said one. "My wife has fallen ill," claimed the other. The third, simulating a coughing fit, blurted out that he was sick. And so, everyone had something.

I was genuinely worried and completely confused. The fishermen have had a good time under my protection and were grateful to me. They belonged to the elite in terms of earnings. I took care of their health and the education of their children. For comfort and safety. This was not selfless: their work was, as I have said, vital to the sustenance of Stanleyville. Therefore, when after many battles I captured the outpost in Wanie Rukula, I directed my main effort to settling with fishing tribes the very fishy section of the Lualaba River that I had liberated. And this was not an easy thing, as the fishermen had fled into the jungle – as did most of the population – and were afraid to return to their lands, frightened by red propaganda about retribution from us for the whites in Stanleyville. Shipped away by the rebels to labor away from their traditional fishing grounds, deprived of their leadership, they wandered through the jungles rampaged about by fear and hunger. They died often and heavily from hunger and disease. Especially children!

I was lucky at the time. During one of the minor pacification operations, my soldiers found an old, exhausted native in the jungle. When he recovered from his fear, he managed to get out of him through an interpreter that he was the head of the M'Wabu fishing tribe, which before the outbreak of the rebellion lived on one of the tributaries of the Congo River. This tribe scattered when the Reds captured the chief. The boss was held hostage deep in the jungle and barely managed to escape. He had been wandering for a long time, hiding from both the rebels and our military. He was close to death when we found him.

With his help, the entire M'Wabu tribe was pulled out of the forest: when the old cacique came back to life and saw that the devil was not so terrible, that we did not murder anyone, and that people lived normally and safely in the liberated territories, he agreed without difficulty to summon his fellow tribesmen to out of hiding. For days the tom-toms sounded the call of the old boss. They proclaimed that he was healthy, that he guaranteed their safety and prosperity. For the next two weeks, scattered M'Wabu families emerged from the jungle. At night, cautiously, like hunted animals, they joined their leader. As they returned, I set them up in an abandoned village at the foot of the outpost. Our proximity protected them from the vengeance of the rebels, who punished them with death for trying to disassociate themselves from their rule. The M'Wabu tribe has long been grateful to me. The old boss made me some sort of honorary chief of the tribe, gave me a girlfriend, and called me his father. The latter, of course, was only symbolic... fortunately!

It was no wonder that the sudden pseudo-strike of the fishermen in M'Wabu came as a surprise to me. I feel something bad is happening. I knew they weren't being honest with me, that they were up to something. Could the rebels have managed to intimidate them? In fact, they looked frightened: huddling in groups, speaking in whispers. From one of the huts came the faint but heartbreaking cry of a woman. I couldn't find out anything specific. The old boss was gone, and no one could or wouldn't tell me what had happened to him. But I had put too much work into organizing the fishing, too many hungry people were waiting for fish for me to give up. As usual in such cases, I sent for Father M.

The irreplaceable priest M.! An expert not only in Negro customs, but also in the Negro soul. Superstitions, witchcraft, and taboos held no secrets for him. He was an invaluable assistant in all matters concerning relations with the natives. And now he stood before me, breathless and helpless. His blue, nearsighted eyes, behind his glasses, expressed utter astonishment.

"It's unheard of, Condottieri," he said. "I'd sooner expect white bears than crocodile men here!"

The second whiskey (before noon!) calmed him down a bit.

"Crocodile people," he began to speak in a calmer tone, "are small cannibal tribes. They travel along the rivers. They rarely number more than a hundred people, including small children. When they come across a fishing village, they lurk in the thickets on the opposite side of the river. They wait until night. You know, Condottieri, what fishing here looks like..."

I did know. I have watched my M'Wabu many times. What a picturesque view! Twenty or thirty canoes come out on the river, with two men in each. They're both standing. One at the back, with a long bamboo pole, propels the canoe, the other at the front, with a torch in his left hand and a javelin in his right, for catching fish... There are so many fish in this river that flocks of them are drawn to the lights. The fisherman strings them on a javelin and throws them into the boat, like a peasant with a pitchfork. Fish from five to ten kilos. In a quarter of an hour the canoe is full... You have to make it to the shore, where the women empty it quickly. New voyage, new hunt. Dozens of torches on the wide-spread waters of the river. The light is reflected in the waves. The moon, palm trees on the shore. How blissful!

"Crocodile men swim underwater," continued Father M. "Two, three, with a bamboo tube in their mouth to breathe. They swim to the canoe farthest from the others, closest to the opposite shore, and overturn it. Besides, a canoe is just a hollowed-out tree trunk. They drown the fishermen, then pull them ashore. After gutting... several dozen kilos of meat. The whole tribe has something to eat. The next day they glide on to another fishing village. And superstitious fishermen believe in impure forces and are afraid to go fishing all day long."

"The Belgian administration of the Congo has been fighting this scourge since the beginning of colonial times," continued Father. M., clearly affected. "And so, I was taught, in the 1920s there were no crocodile men in the Congo."

How thin is the polish of civilization! In the 1960s, a short moment was enough for decades of civilizational work to be forgotten and old habits to be revived.

Cannibalism still exists in Africa... Sometimes it is ritual cannibalism. The liver of a defeated enemy is eaten to usurp his valor. But simple cannibalism for food also exists. Well, sometimes it's easier to hunt a man than an antelope... Two years before the reported events, northeast of Stanleyville, a plane had crashed into the jungle. It was flown, in addition to the crew, by twelve Italian technicians. In the jungle, cut off from the rest of the army, a Congolese infantry battalion was starving. Only the gnawed bones were left after they found the crew of the plane and the Italian technicians. The world media has been silent about this fact. To speak of cannibalism is to be accused of racism. Especially when the right to self-determination of "nations" is supported.

I felt a spasm in my throat with disgust, I held back the overpowering desire to "drive to Riga." In the clearing - on the right side of the Lualaba River - a battlefield! Corpses of naked men and women. The putrid stench makes you sick. Accompanied by the old chief of the M'Wabu tribe, we see what the day before was the camp of the "crocodile people." An extinguished bonfire; above it, on two crosses, a rod serving as a barbecue spit, and around uneaten human remains. Cut off heads in the grass. The heads of men I knew: two M'Wabu fishermen.

After talking to Father M., I sent companies of Katangese soldiers with orders to kill the cannibals. It wasn't fair. Can someone be punished for behaving in accordance with his customs? But I was faced with the necessity of providing my fishermen with the peaceful fishing on which the sustenance of the city depended. The "Crocodile Men" were killed by Katangese bullets. The old chief of the fishing tribe found out by sight that it was not the evil spirits of the night that were waiting for his subordinates.

In the evening, amidst the weeping of women and children, to the gloomy sound of tom-toms, the village of Wanie Rukula held a funeral of two heads. That night, dozens of torches shone on the majestic river.

Oh, that eternal Africa...

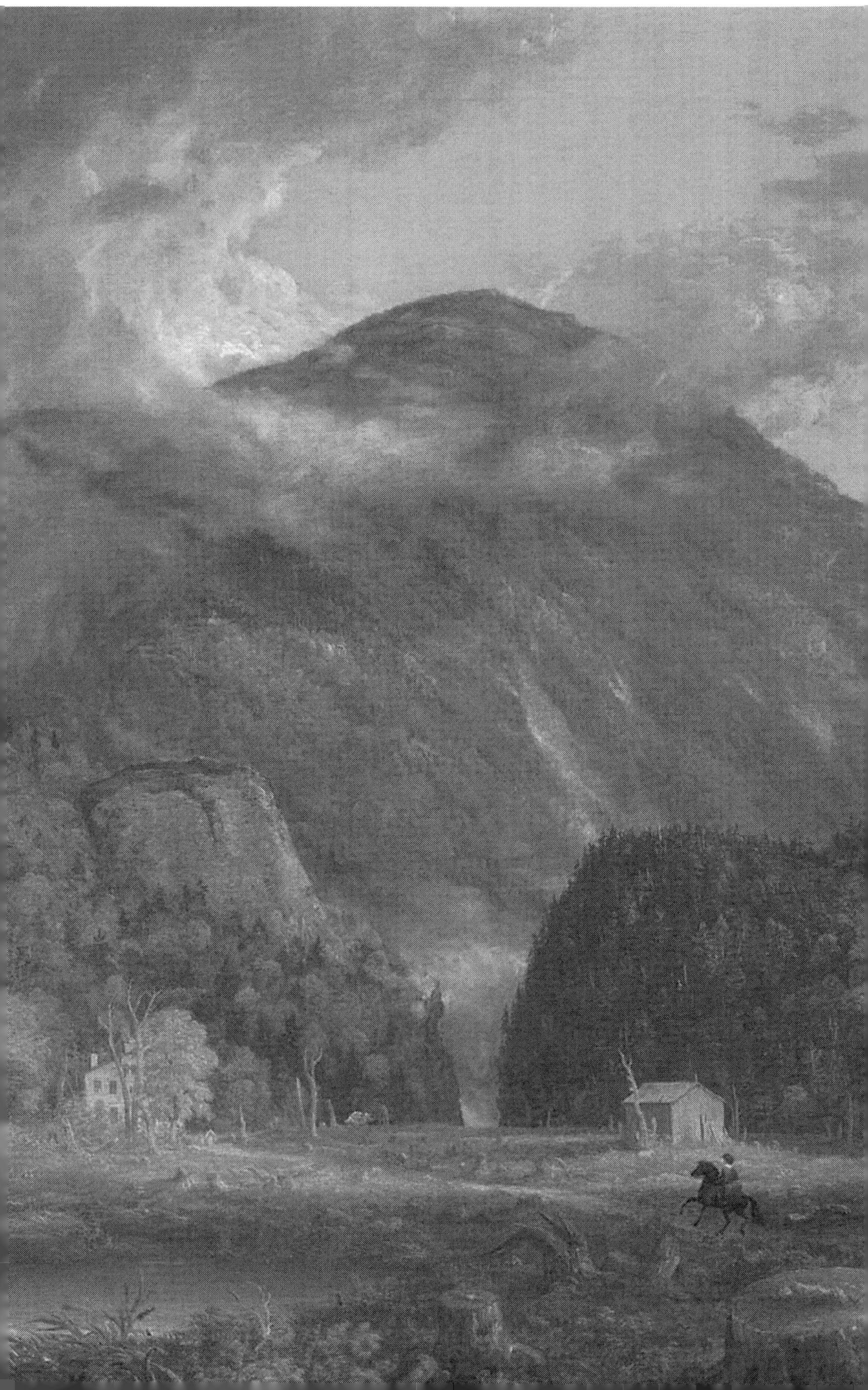

The Trauma of the Frontier

By Rupert August

Settlement of the open Frontier is typically not as popular as its reputation, and the romance surrounding it might suggest. The people who try to settle or tame them often have no choice, usually because they are unable to make a life in their original home. The frontier is then a punishment, or a refuge from some kind of persecution or pursuit, or simply the last option when no others are available.

The exception to this is a man – an aristocrat usually – who dabbles in the frontier as a kind of hobby or adventure, content in the knowledge that he may return home at any time. For him, the frontier is a curiosity, or a canvas on which he can sketch out his ideals, but mostly at a comfortable distance from real tribulations. This was particularly true of the Americas, where the original 13 colonies were made up of a combination of rejects from the mother country (for having the wrong religious beliefs or political affiliations), or simply poor vagabonds shipped off as labor. These groups were managed by notables who were likewise troublesome enough at home to be given a polity abroad to run: men like the Lockeans of Carolina, William Penn in Pennsylvania, or James Oglethorpe in Georgia. Later, during the Highland Clearances, many Highland Scots were given little option between trying to figure out life on their own in some new locality, or a one-way ticket to Canada after their eviction.

More recently still, Australia was run as a penal colony – but with the additional wrinkle that conditions in the newly swelled cities in the UK could be bad enough that some would deliberately commit a minor crime and get caught so as to be given a free ticket to somewhere they might have a chance of better living. None of these were intrepid wanderers, conquerors, or adventurers; this usually only occurs once there is something established to join, rather than something to found.

Leaving the Anglo context, it remains somewhat similar. Residence in Rome was almost always preferred when possible, but at times the poverty and conditions could be crushing enough that joining a newly founded colonia might be a better alternative. Likewise – although sometimes a measure to combat overcrowding – mass exile, displacement, and the forming of a new colony or Polis in Ancient Greece was at least as often used as a punishment. Even Carthage was formed by a sect of religious fanatics, too radical for their fellow Phoenicians. In all of these cases, home was preferable, but impossible.

The times where this does not apply are curious in themselves: where there already exists some kind of society to join, and even better if it is as a new aristocracy; alternatively, if there is an existing empire to plunder and partition. Particularly, this applies in India and among the Conquistadors – both rather temporary phenomena. Granted, the original Conquistadors could not have fully known what they were signing up for when they enlisted with Albuquerque, Cortés, or Pizzaro; but they were all able to extract all the benefits and treasures of empires in only a few years.

Even presented with the fantastical wealth available trapping for pelts in Siberia and Canada, settlement generally had to be managed and encouraged before more than a handful of nefarious characters would accept the offer. Similarly, once the original Spanish conquests had already happened and the New World Colonies were already established, the quality of Spaniards which could be attracted to live there was so low as to make regulation of the slave trade, and improved treatment of the natives, to be impossible tasks. Anyone who can even passingly 'make it' in the home country, would rather do so.

When the United States had already been established with bustling cities, and plenty of ready-made social infrastructure that a newcomer might easily slip into, it's said that anywhere up to 25% of immigrants later left to return home. The pull of the native soil and the comfort of home is powerful indeed.

Instead, then, a move to the frontier is all too often an act of desperation and despair. A tragedy which is to be borne, rather than an exciting opportunity; an abandonment of hope, and sometimes a feeling of rejection by the home that they love. This is not a fate to be embraced prematurely, but all the same it may be necessary, or even already with us today. As with civil wars, there are certainly some stories of triumph and glory, but the overriding experience is one of grief.

And yet the alternative is much worse. Even if one's progeny are forced or allowed to return to the native land, it may seem foreign after the new climes of the Frontier have imprinted themselves. Consider many of the Loyalists of the American Revolution who loved England, but could not live there when given refuge and encouraged to settle after the war. Many made their peace with the treasonous colonies, and went back to live in the lands of their birth. One is molded by the Frontier; in equal measure to how it is tamed, it unwinds those who inhabit it.

In the frame of Turchin, this process is necessary for the preservation and renewal of civilization. When the core has become dysfunctional and the prime stock has degenerated, with a useless or counterproductive ruling elite, the men of the borderlands and Frontiers are required to restabilize.

Invariably they will be treated as barbarians, even as they ascend to rule. These may be of the original stock, or of a new stock, so typically – for the sake of not being ruled by foreigners – having a readily available cadre to fill the role is most ideal. For Rome it was the Soldier Emperors; for Byzantium, the Isaurians among others; for Egypt, an unending chain of conquerors from Assyria; to the Achaemenids, the Greeks, Romans, and on and on it goes. The Egyptians are a sad reminder of what might befall a people who are too insular and urbanized. Granted, it is less clear how this phenomenon of the restoring barbarism interacts with modernity, but with one level of reduction; the core observation of a synthesis of modern technologies and systems, with older clear-sightedness, and an unpretentious attitude towards what must be done, is clearly applicable.

On one hand, then, we have the pain of estrangement, and on the other we have the necessary rejection of frills and pretense. A personal sacrifice must be made, not even for the guarantee of a future duty to be fulfilled, but merely the possibility. A grim ask indeed, when put into these terms – and hence, something done out of necessity rather than choice in most cases. If we had a foresighted and sympathetic ruler, or even cadre of powerful supporters, we might be able to create these frontiersmen in other ways, such as generous patronage and sponsorship, but the price seems prohibitively high. It is not enough to have mercantile support to meet costs; the wealth and power of Princes and Tsars is necessary for the Cossack option to be viable. There will likely be no Yermak, no Cossack host funded by aristocratic interests and the Tsar; only open space, and whatever one's own muscle can acquire. Perhaps, like the Roman Illyrians, a call will be heard to lead and serve again. Perhaps, like the American Loyalists, the Frontier itself will be subverted, and such men will be thrown back into their homeland adrift and unfit for their surroundings. Perhaps, like the Cossacks, the core will be turned against them, and they will be purged and slaughtered. Or, like the Australians, their efforts will simply bring another locality under the purview and rule of the Empire, while the frontiersmen themselves wither in number and ethic, forgotten.

Modernizing all this any further creates more problems. When near-enough the entire planet can be monitored, has already been mapped, and has the ability to tap into the cosmopolis at will via the internet, can there ever be another Frontiersman? It's an open question, and perhaps the decay will continue infinitely, with no ability for an outside force to reimpose order, other than cruel nature herself. Such a scenario, while plausible, is much more apocalyptic. So instead let the question be answered by how this despair of exile now manifests.

There is no shortage of heresies which need to be purged by the core, but their exile is now much more digital. Some are forced abroad as well, but not to an uninhabited periphery. Instead, like the exile of Imperial Russia, the modern heretic must simply stay away from the core of the worldwide Cosmopolis. A second-rate country will do, perhaps even a second-rate city. He must make do with second-rate services (as understood by the elite of the core, not necessarily inferior in practice), and his name is a byword for vice in the mainstream rhetoric. And although this (primarily digital) exile is partly functional as a stand-in for the frontiersman archetype, there is a lack of the same weight of loss, because so much of the pretense, luxury, and comfort remain available. The soil beneath one's feet can often remain one's own, which in itself is a comfort which can make one fearful of loss, where a more pragmatic man might recognize the need and opportunity to act. The Afrikaaners may not have embarked on their Great Trek if they had been merely socially estranged in the Netherlands, in recognition of what they still might lose. To truly embrace the Frontier ethic, as the Afrikaaners seem to, it may be necessary to be almost totally estranged, perhaps even keeping only the blood inheritance, replacing all else with a pragmatism that follows grieving what else has been lost.

I do not necessarily advocate this path myself, because indeed I do not walk it myself. But if the promise of the Frontier, and the Mannerbund of Restoration is to be taken seriously, it cannot be half-hearted, and comfortable, with one foot in both worlds. It must be total, and passing over that threshold will incur grief, pain, and struggle. If it is survived, the prizes are superiority and worthiness, awaiting an opportunity.

BROUGHT TO YOU BY THE DISSIDENT REVIEW

@DISSIDENT_REV

DISSIDENTREVIEW.COM

COVER ART BY ███████ ███████